Roland Legrand

The art of forecasting

with astrology

Painting by Anne-Laure Dauny
https://lacerisecosmique.jimdofree.com

© ABLAS astrology - March 2021

Foreword

THE ART OF FORECASTING WITH ASTROLOGY

Millions of people across the globe regularly consult fortune-tellers, psychics, clairvoyants, and astrologers. It seems that knowing what the future holds helps to better accept life's circumstances by offering a broader and more philosophical view of earthly existence.

Sceptics consider esoteric arts as sheer superstitions and blind beliefs that have no rational basis whatsoever. For them, it is ridiculous to pretend predicting the future because all events are coincidental.

To illustrate this, I took the liberty of copying for you two definitions of astrology found in the "Petit Larousse illustré", a popular French dictionary. The first one is from the 1918 edition and the second one from the 1986 version.

1918's definition:

"ASTROLOGY: The art of foreseeing events from the observation of the planets. This chimerical science claimed to predict the future according to the movements of the planets, as if they could have an influence on events that solely depend on free will.

Born in Chaldea, astrology was brought to Egypt, then to Greece, Italy and throughout the Western World. It is difficult to believe that the most famous men of all times, such as Tacit, Galileo, Saint Thomas d'Acquin, Tycho-Brahe, Kepler and a thousand more were fervent adepts of astrology. In ancient times, each Prince had an astrologer at his court. That of Louis XI was called Galeotti, and that of Catherine de Medici was Come Ruggieri, both Italians. Not a person of importance was born without calling an astrologer to draw up their horoscope. This absurd superstition did not completely disappear until the 17th century. "

No comment ...

The 1986 edition is shorter and more neutral.

"ASTROLOGY: Divinatory art seeking to determine the influence of the planets on the course of terrestrial events to draw various predictions and forecasts."

In this second definition, we can feel that the author was reluctant to develop more on the subject ...

All events in our life seem mostly self-created, consciously, or unconsciously. Hence, it is quite simple to predict a car accident to an impatient driver or a heart attack to a person suffering from cardiovascular deficiency and high blood pressure ... From these simple facts, it is highly probable that some unlucky day the driver will have an accident and the person with a heart condition will suffer from complications.

The question is: "how does astrology fit here?"

Fast drivers are usually nervous and irritable people. Impatient and impulsive, they cannot control their need to overtake other cars, driving as if they were always in great hurry.

Astrology clearly shows such tendencies in the person's birth chart. It may be because of the Ascendant in Aries, because of Mars, Uranus, or Pluto in discordance with Jupiter or Mercury in relation to House III. There may also be conflicting aspects involving the Moon and Uranus, the Sun, or the Ascendant. There are multiple configurations that can explain nervousness that manifests itself behind the steering wheel in a car. However, to analyse a birth chart is not enough to forecast an accident-prone period.

The same applies to the person with cardiovascular deficiency. House VI in Leo with the Sun afflicted by Mars, Saturn, or Uranus may indicate such health condition. Other planetary configurations may confirm the above, but as numerous as they can be, they are not sufficient to forecast periods during which a heart attack or other related complications may happen.

The study of the potential influences of the movements of the planets around the birth chart is the key to forecasting such events.

In this book, I describe and explain how to read what planetary transits have in store for us. This is a rather easy and effective technique to make short and long-term simple astrological previsions. Like anything else, the more you practice, the better you become. Astrology is an art. As such, it requires dedication, motivation and passion to master it.

What you need to have to make this book useful and pratical

- A book of Ephemeris (also called Ephemerides) in which the daily positions of the planets and other elements are listed. Visit this website to get access to nine thousand years of ephemeris for free:

https://www.astro.com/swisseph/swepha_f.htm

- The birth chart of the person concerned (you or someone else)

What you need to know

- The energy principles represented by the elements in the chart.[1]

- The symbolism of each Sign and House.

- The relationship between planets, Signs and Houses

- The rulership of each planet

- The values of the major aspects (conjunction, sextile, square, trine, inconjunct, and opposition).

If you cannot master the above, get my **"Astrology for a Better life"** book available from the Amazon website in your country.

What you must do

- Place the chart to be analysed conveniently in front of you.

- Prepare the ephemeris for the period you want information about.

---

[1] I use the word "element" to relate to any of the eight planets, the Sun, the Moon, and two asteroids, Vesta and Chiron.

- Choose the period (month/year or even day/month/year) depending on the object of your research.

- Draw the symbols of the elements in transit at suitable places around the chart where they form relevant aspects with the natal positions of the planets and other elements (ASC. MC. Etc.) in the chart concerned.

- Analyse the different configurations.

Whether you are new to astrology or have been practicing for several years, what you read in this book will help you to improve your technique or simply discover how far astrology can go when it is used appropriately. The most accurate forecast must be your only goal and motivation.

In order of appearance in this book, I cover the possible effects of Jupiter, Saturn, Chiron, Uranus, Neptune, and Pluto forming various transiting aspects with natal positions of important elements in a birth chart. There is a large section dedicated to their possible effects on the cusp and while they transit the Houses. I have also included the faster transits of the Sun, the Moon, Mercury, Venus, Mars and Vesta in the Houses and their triggering action on slower transits. You will also find interesting information about Lilith and the Lunar Nodes.

Use this book, do not just read it. It is meant as a course. That is why I have called each chapter a "lesson". There are twenty-one of them. Practice each lesson before studying the next one.

Thank you for your interest in astrology and in my work.

Roland Legrand
March 2021

Lesson 1

WHAT IS A TRANSIT?

A *transit* is the movement or displacement of a planet or other object and element (lunar node, Lilith, Vesta, Chiron and more) around a chart (usually a birth chart).

Why and how does a transit affect us?

The planets are continually moving, progressing around the Sun, therefore, from our point of view on Earth, around the zodiac. The fixity of their positions on the drawing of a birth chart can be compared to a photograph. Just as the picture of a newborn can be taken and later compared to another, the transits are representative of the effect of time between two chosen moments in life. The photo of the newborn will never change, but the newborn will change every day, always in relation with the original image.

As you know, the positions of the planets at birth are recorded around the "horoscope" or "natal chart". They form the basic framework for the elaboration of a person's destiny. It is true for everyone. The psychological portrait provided by our astrological identity card is precise and detailed. The natal chart is an energetic imbroglio that continues to influence us until the end of life. Gradual or sudden changes in this complex web are produced by planetary transits, with the faster moving planets acting as detonators to the energies produced by the slower ones ...

How a transit affects life depends primarily on the planet or other element involved and of its importance in the birth chart.

There are two categories of transits:

- "Slow transits"
- "Fast transits"

The "fast transits" are those of the Moon, the Sun, Mercury, Venus, Mars, and the asteroid Vesta that I consider as ruler of Libra in my practice of astrology since 1998.

The effect of a fast transit is of short duration and sometimes difficult to associate with specific events. They often serve in more remarkable manner as detonators of latent energies derived from the transits of slow planets.

The most significant transiting aspect, the one with the most obvious influence, is *the conjunction*. It forms when a moving planet passes at the longitude of an element in the birth chart.[2]

When a planet in transit returns to its natal position, also called *radical position*, it seems to have a stronger influence. It can be perceived in a change in behaviour, as well as in the events that take place in the areas of life represented by the planet and other elements involved. The return of a planet determines the end of a cycle in relation to the rulership of the planet in the birth chart. It also naturally indicates the beginning of a new cycle that will last until the planet concerned returns once more.

The moon's time of revolution around the Earth and around the zodiac is the shortest with only 27 days and 6 hours. By comparison, Pluto's revolution time around the zodiac is 248 years and by far the longest of all celestial object in the solar system.

Studying transits and mastering the analysis of their effects will take much longer in terms of personal practice than the time needed to read this book. It is designed to explain the "ABLAS method" through repeated practical use. This is how you will become a genuine forecaster or a professional astrologer ...

To embark on the study of the art of forecasting with astrology, we will discuss the influence of the *conjunction* and, more particularly, the returns of planets to their radical positions, beginning with the slower planets, from Jupiter to Uranus. Due to their extremely slow speed, Neptune and Pluto cannot return to their original positions in

---

[2] An "element" is a planet, the cusp of a House, the Moon, the Sun, the lunar nodes, and any object present around the birth chart.

a chart during a human lifetime. Neptune needs 165 years and Pluto 248 years...

The transiting conjunctions of Neptune and Pluto with radical planets, House cusps, and other elements in the birth chart are however very important. They will be discussed in future chapters of this book.

The "*slow*" transits are those of Jupiter, Saturn, Chiron, Uranus, Neptune, and Pluton.

The other transiting aspects (sextiles, squares, trines, inconjuncts, and oppositions) are, to my knowledge, much less influential than the conjunction.

Slow transits have a more profound and long-lasting influence than fast transits.

Slow dissonant transits have an influence that often progressively become imperceptible. It may even be possible to control the energy of a dissonant slow transit and use it favourably rather than remain a victim of it. During these long periods, faster transits serve as detonators of events generated by slow transits.

Neptune and Pluto are so slow that they have an influence on whole generations. Yet their effects are very deep individually through their House positions and the aspects involving various elements in someone's birth chart.

Transiting conjunctions with important elements of a birth chart often coincide with major events, deep questioning, renewed confusion, or the opportunity for a fresh start in the areas represented by the planets involved and the Houses they rule.

These events depend on fast transits to be triggered. Free will, however, can intervene to modify, amplify, favour, or block the potential influence of a transiting conjunction.

In the next lessons, we will debate on the possible effects of slow planets, from Jupiter to Pluto.

Lesson 2

The slow planets

Jupiter

♃

Here is a scientific article, written by Henry T. Simmons in the "Science and Future" supplement to the Encyclopedia Britannica about the space missions of Pioneer 10 and Pioneer 11 in the vicinity of Jupiter. It is worthy of interest in this lesson.

Pioneer 10 recorded an optimal bombardment of 13 million electrons per square centimetre per second in an energy radius of over 50 million electron volts (MeV). The total electron flow on Pioneer 10 reached much higher levels, but the 50 MeV of particles, capable of penetrating several centimetres of brass, represented the greatest danger in electron bombardment for the spacecraft ...

The intense radiation storm shut down many of the scientific instruments on board the ship and seriously interfered with its work when it was close to the planet. During the two weeks that Pioneer 10 spent in the vicinity of Jupiter, it was subjected to a dose of radiation several thousand times greater than the lethal dose for humans ... The two vessels (Pioneer 10 and Pioneer 11) encountered electron flows of Jovian origin when they were more than 140 million kilometres from the planet ...

How could such radiation flow not reach us on Earth in an invisible but very real manner?

This is a question that automatically comes to mind when you read this kind of article while studying astrology. Unfortunately, astronomers or astrophysicists no longer venture into astrological research. They prefer to leave it to those who dedicate their lives to the study of cosmic influences on our planet and its "tenants". Unfortunately, astrologers often lack basic knowledge in astronomy, so useful to complement and give more credibility to their reasoning.

Each planet in the solar system has a magnetic field derived from its constitution and other complex factors.

The Sun, for example, is made up of about 88% hydrogen and 11% helium. Jupiter is very close to it, with a composition of around 82% hydrogen and 17% helium.

We all know the importance of the Sun as giver of life on Earth. The powerful energy of Jupiter rivals with that of the Sun to create a blend that allows life to spread and to grow. The Sun is life, while Jupiter is growth...

Because the Sun's constitution and type of radiation are similar to Jupiter's, we can compare the transits of the giant planet to those of the Sun. However, Jupiter's revolution around the zodiac is twelve times slower than the Sun's apparent course in one year. The slower speed means that Jupiter stays twelve times longer than the Sun in the same sector of the zodiac. Hence, its energy field penetrates deeper during its transits around a birth chart. Jupiter spends an average of one year in each sign. The Sun travels the same distance of 30° in one month ...

Therefore, if Jupiter's influence resembles that of the Sun it would thus be rather beneficial and vital. The Sun is the giver of life. It also helps to maintain it, but it can deteriorate it and make it difficult when it is predominant or too strong. This is the case in the desert, for example, where heat and solar radiations are particularly unsafe for all life forms.

The Jovian influence is said to bring wealth and happiness, but it can also become destructive in many ways.

All planetary influences have their opposite expressed according to their initial positions in the chart. The same principle applies during transits when they form various aspects with the elements present around the birth chart.

THE CONJUNCTION

Approximate ages. Please, verify in the ephemeris.

	Sextile	Square	Trine	Opposition	Inconjunct	Conjunction
	2 - 10	3 - 9	4 - 8	6	5	12
	14 - 22	15 - 21	16 - 20	18	7	24
					17	36
AGE	26 - 34	27 - 33	28 - 32	30	19	48
	38 - 46	39 - 45	40 - 44	42	29	59-60
					31	71
	50 - 58	51 - 57	52 - 56	54	41	83
	62 - 70	63 - 69	64 - 68	66	43	95
					53	Etc.
	74 - 82	75 - 81	76 - 80	78	55	
	Etc.	Etc.	Etc.	Etc.	Etc.	

From birth, Jupiter returns to its original position every twelve years or so when it creates a transiting conjunction with its own position in the chart. This aspect seems to reinforce the influence of Jupiter in the areas it represents (the House beginning in Sagittarius) and is the areas represented by the House where it is found in the birth chart.

The return of Jupiter signals the end of a cycle and the beginning of a new one that will last for precisely 11 years and 315 days. Jupiter's cycles are what I call *"cycles of evolution"*. The events and experiences lived during one cycle should therefore be beneficial or at least useful to derive more from the ensuing one.

All aspects involving Jupiter in the birth chart regain energy and are more noticeable for the duration of the transiting conjunction (from several months to a whole year).

The period is marked by multiple opportunities. Their quality and importance depend on the aspects involving Jupiter in the birth chart combined with the transits of other planets during the same period.

A transiting conjunction of Jupiter with its own position in the chart is usually beneficial, but it relies on the other aspects produced by other planets in transit during the period concerned. Jupiter's transiting influence is transferred through the chart where it enhances positive character traits and latent potentials in the areas represented by the planets involved that are subject to the powerful energy of the giant planet.

Sextiles and trines are beneficial aspects.

The sextile enhances latent potentials, and the trine enhances optimism and enthusiasm, with happy repercussions on behaviour and on personal or social achievements.

Jupiter forming harmonious transiting aspects with its own position is said to bring luck, opportunities, progress, evolution, and success.

However, the chart must be examined to determine in what areas of life and to what degree the Jovian influence expresses itself during a transit.

From a purely symbolic point of view, since Jupiter represents the principle of expansion, the sectors concerned are subject to a period of evolution and progress. At the same time, Jupiter can produce a tendency to take things for granted rather than act judiciously to make the most out of various opportunities.

It also happens that the transit of Jupiter in a House increases the problems encountered in the areas of life represented by that House. Aspects with the ruler of the House concerned must be analysed to forecast the possible effect of Jupiter during such a transit, knowing that it can last from a few months to more than one year[3] ...

More commonly, the sectors of life represented by the House where Jupiter transits benefit from some degree of growth and evolution. The House becomes an area of potential success and rejoicing. Simultaneously, the aspects Jupiter makes with planets and other elements in the birth chart, as well as the Houses concerned, must be taken into consideration.

---

[3] The duration of a transit through a House depends on its size or width.

Every twelve years or so, a cycle of evolution ends and a new one begins. The first conjunction occurs at 12 years of age, the second at 24, the third at 36, and so on until the end of life. See the chart on the first page of this chapter for more details.

Note that the return of Jupiter in the sign it occupied at birth generally corresponds to the Chinese zodiac sign year. If you are a Tiger, every twelve years will be "your" year, a period often marked by great events in relation with your aspirations and ambitions. When you turn 60, the original element (Fire, for example) reoccurs. There are five elements in Chinese astrology: 5 x 12 = 60.

Significant events are likely to mark the ensuing twelve-year cycle. The forecast must be organised around the sectors represented by Jupiter in the birth chart (House in Sagittarius) and the sectors represented by the House where Jupiter was at birth.

For example, if Jupiter represents House II and is in House X in the birth chart, each time it returns to its natal sign and House, a period of professional improvement and career opportunities are to be expected with positive consequences on finances and revenues.

Without having to refer to the ephemeris, work out the next time (year) Jupiter returns to its original position in your birth chart. It is quite easy to assess because Jupiter takes almost one year to transit through each sign.

For example, if it is in Virgo in your birth chart, count how many signs Jupiter needs to transit to reach Virgo from its position in sign when you read this. The result is the number of years you will have to wait.

Note that due to retrogradation periods, Jupiter, alike other planets, can be held for several months in the same area of the zodiac. Travelling through a sign, it enters the following one, then retreats into the previous one before it returns to the next sign again.

To found out more about retrogradations, read "Astrology for a Better Life. Teach yourself and practice". The book is available from Amazon in your region or from your local bookstore.

Once you determine the next return of Jupiter in your birth chart, check which areas of life will be most affected by this important cosmic event.

Simultaneously, based on the position of Jupiter in your birth chart, see which sectors are linked to this planet. These sectors will benefit from a serious boost every twelve years, a period marked by new opportunities for evolution, growth, and success.

Such influence seems to be more particularly noticeable at the age of 36, when the "age of Jupiter" begins, a time of professional and social evolution that depends on personal objectives, latent potentials, and drive to succeed. This "Jovian" period lasts until Saturn's second return on its original position, at 59, when many of us prepare for retirement and for Saturn's third cycle that will last until the eighty-seventh birthday ...

What happens if during such a transit a square or opposition involves Jupiter with Saturn in the birth chart?

The latent influence of difficult aspects in the natal chart seems to diminish during the beneficial transits of Jupiter, whether it is a transiting conjunction, a sextile, or a trine.

Those periods are usually marked by opportunities to overcome the obstacles represented by a natal opposition between Jupiter and Saturn, and thus gain ground in the face of adversity.

It is also a favourable period to counterbalance the effect of the opposition between these two planets, often representative of difficult experiences during childhood or adolescence, when transiting Saturn forms a square with the opposition with Saturn (around the age of seven) and when it forms a transiting conjunction with Jupiter, opposite its own position (around the age of fourteen or fifteen).

Squares and oppositions produce existential ups and downs, which are detrimental to the pursuit of goals and to success. It is often only during Saturn's second return, around the age of 59, that a happy "in-between" is found. Life's circumstances then encourage prudence and allow a more pleasant and harmonious third cycle than the first and second ones ...

The Jupiter / Saturn opposition seems to have a strong incidence on the pursuit of financial goals. It indicates a tendency to be torn apart between ambitious projects and lack of motivation. Periods of abundance are followed by periods of scarcity. There is a degree of inadequacy in managing finances. Life may be pulled between a tendency to eat too much and the need for a strict diet. The alternance usually lasts until middle age when, finally understanding life's lessons, a happy middle-way is found. The future becomes brighter and more promising, both morally and materially.

Note that this is an example, not a systematic incidence of the opposition between Jupiter and Saturn in a birth chart.

During a harmonic transit, Jupiter boosts optimism, favours better health, and improves personal magnetism, while increasing creativity and objectivity useful to deal with life's challenges derived from interferences from simultaneous transiting aspects.

Regrettably, abundance often results in using Jupiter's positive influence on trivial pursuits of fugacious pleasures rather than on more useful objectives to improve life durably. Jupiter also produces opportunism, a human trait often responsible for various excesses at the expense of constructive energy.

The whole chart provides information on strength of character and the ability to take full advantage (or not) of favourable situations. By knowing yourself better, you learn to manage your life better. On this subject, astrology is considerably useful, you know that.

When Jupiter is strong in the birth chart and beneficial, the person's life path is favoured and protected. For example, Jupiter trine Midheaven (MC) is often found in the charts of personalities from all social backgrounds who brilliantly succeed socially, artistically, or otherwise.

When is Jupiter "strong"?

- In its own sign (Sagittarius).
- When it rules the Ascendant or the sun sign (Sagittarius)
- When it is the dominant planet according to the planetary-chain technique taught in the book *"Astrology for a better life, teach yourself and practise"* mentioned earlier.
- When it is in the Ascendant, in the Midheaven, or in House IX, of which Jupiter is the "natural ruler".
- When it is conjunct the Sun or the Moon.
- When it forms a conjunction, sextile, or trine with the ruler of the Sun sign or the Ascendant.

There are other factors that can be determined according to the chart to be analysed. This stronger influence of Jupiter manifests itself during its harmonious transits by enhancing the outcomes derived from the opportunities fostered by the positive energy of this powerful planet.

After the transiting conjunction, comes the next aspect, the sextile.

THE SEXTILE

The sextile is a harmonic aspect that links signs belonging to compatible elements. They are spontaneously complementary. Fire and Air, Earth and Water are compatible and complementary elements. It becomes a source of active energy in the case of Fire and Air, and of constructive energy in the case of Earth and Water.

During a transiting sextile with its own position or with other elements of the birth chart, Jupiter favours a positive evolution of projects through a flow of dynamic and productive motivation.

The two transiting sextiles occurring during the complete revolution of a planet around the zodiac have different functions. The first one precedes a square, while the second precedes a half-sextile.

In the first case, the favourable period during the transiting sextile should be viewed like "the calm before the storm". The positive outcome of the transiting sextile should be used to prepare for the following transit and thus better manage the period of the square.

After the second sextile comes the half-sextile, traditionally considered to be harmonic. Therefore, it could be advised not to worry too much about a less cheerful tomorrow than with the square. However, I have a different point of view ...

About the half-sextile

The half-sextile is a connection between two signs belonging to incompatible elements. They are Fire and Water, Air and Earth, Air and Water, Fire and Earth. We find the same associations in the square aspect, known as being dissonant. Therefore, I consider the sextile to be more dissonant than beneficial. While all signs are interrelated with their immediate counterparts, they are nonetheless out of tune with them. This applies for the following and preceding signs.

For example, believing that Pisces is in harmonious or complementary relationship with Aries because they are neighbours is simplistic and inappropriate. Obviously, they have a very different type of energy. You do not need much knowledge in astrology to understand this.

Likewise, Aries is different from Taurus, which is different from Gemini, and so on. These differences cohabit around the zodiac to form its richness and diversity.

The half-sextile is situated between the sextile and the conjunction, a position that makes it a transitional aspect. This ambiguous situation is also found in the effect of the quincunx (inconjunct) which, alike the square and half-sextile, connects signs that belong to incompatible elements.

Back to the sextile

Here is some useful information to help you analyse sextiles. They relate to transiting Jupiter in aspect with its initial position in the birth chart.

The first sextile occurs at two years of age, when Jupiter reaches a sixty-degree angle with its own position in the birth chart. It should be a pleasant time when the child's abilities are asserted and developing fast. Speech, motion management, and cleanliness are some of the little-one's progress.

The second sextile

The second sextile occurs at ten years of age, when the child is undergoing academic, social, and moral development. The youngster becomes aware of earthly realities, such as the notions of justice and injustices.

The third sextile

The third sextile occurs two years after Jupiter's first return to its original position, at the age of 14, a period when Saturn is about to form the first opposition with its original position.

The sextile of Jupiter softens the influence of Saturn and favours the emergence of the first love and intimate relationship. Dreams of becoming a star or of other grandiose success mark this exceptionally interesting and important period of life.

Adolescence has a reputation for being a difficult phase. This is best understood by analysing the effect of the transit of Saturn, which we will discuss a little later in this book. Moreover, this second sextile formed by transiting Jupiter with its original position in the chart leads, like the first one, to a square (discordant) aspect, a year later.

The fourth sextile

The fourth sextile occurs at 22. It precedes the conjunction which takes place two years later, at 24. The opportunities during this period are of course taken advantage of in a more mature fashion than at the age of 10, during the previous sextile preceding the first conjunction, the first return of Jupiter to its original position.

It is a period marked by important projects, when young adulthood allows to get involved in life more concretely, including studies that encourage future involvements in far-fetched projects. Ambition is not the only source of achievement. Work, patience, and determination represented by Saturn are put forward in a more rational and concrete manner. Realism and ambition are major challenges at 24 when transiting Saturn is forming a square (discordant) aspect with its original position.

The other sextiles

For other periods of transiting Jupiter forming sextiles with its initial position, a little common sense should allow you to analyse them and relate them to events or situations you can remember. Observe your birth chart to compare it with Jupiter's transiting sextiles formed with its own position since you were born. They will certainly be relevant of memorable events and periods of evolution in various areas of your life.

THE SQUARE

As with the sextile and the half-sextile, two squares occur during Jupiter's complete journey around the zodiac. The first occurs at 3 years of age, the second at 9, the third at 15, the fourth at 21, etc.

Note that the first square precedes a trine, while the second announces a sextile. In essence, it means that there is much to be learned from these transiting squares (discordant aspects) to give the subsequent beneficial transits a better chance to be favourable.

The square produces excesses in the areas of life represented by Jupiter in the birth chart, and those represented by the House where Jupiter transits.

During such periods, depending on age and circumstances, we are usually tempted to spend more than we earn. We can also get involved in projects or activities that are too ambitious. During a transiting square of Jupiter with its initial position the period can be compromised by serious financial difficulties.

Optimism quickly gives way to bitterness, envy, jealousy, or other negative feeling, fluctuating between euphoria and despair, between disproportionate optimism and lack of self-confidence.

Tastes and aspirations are distorted by Jupiter's magnifying-glass effect. Eating and drinking too much, talking too much, or getting involved in extravagant projects are some of the potential consequences of the influence of a discordant transit of Jupiter with its own position in a chart. Health may also be affected, depending on general condition before the transit.

During such a transiting aspect (which can last for a year), the expansion principle represented by Jupiter feeds on our weaknesses, as well as on our psychological and physiological vulnerability. This is a time when a constant effort is required to approach life's events and situations cautiously, unhurriedly, and thoughtfully to avoid annoying and costly mistakes!

The problems generated by a dissonant transit of Jupiter with its initial position are often triggered by faster transits. Those of Mars and the Moon, for example, play the role of "detonator". We will discuss this phenomenon later in this book.

The transiting square must be analysed while taking into consideration other transits and the elements of information collected in the natal chart, to allow proper assessment of the risks associated with the effect of transiting Jupiter.

Knowing that Jupiter's influence can last for up to one year requires a careful approach to the prognosis. Never forget that the energy developed by this planet is considerably stronger than any other in the solar system.

THE TRINE

Jupiter's transiting trines are very interesting and usually quite favourable to the evolution of life in the areas represented by this planet in the birth chart. The trine seems to neutralize the effects of possible dissonances between *radical*[4] Jupiter and other elements in the chart. The sextile plays a similar role, with a less pronounced manner than the trine according to traditional astrology.

With a trine, talents and potentials are expressed spontaneously and in an efficient and satisfying way. This type of transit also seems to increase the luck factor in the areas represented by Jupiter in the birth chart (House in Sagittarius) and in those related to the House where it transits (House in Aries or Leo depending on the type of trine). It promotes opportunities and their happy consequences. Evolution and success often occur during this kind of beneficial transit.

Note that the effect can last for a whole year with moments of greater intensity when the transiting trine approaches the perfect aspect of 120°.

----

[4] Radical Jupiter = Jupiter at birth. The original position of a planet in the birth chart is said to be "radical".

The first transiting trine with Jupiter's initial position in the chart occurs at 4 years of age, the second at 8, the third at 16, the fourth at 20, the fifth at 28, and so on.

Although it should be analysed together with other simultaneous slow transits, Jupiter's positive effect is usually synonym of protection if not evolution or success. Check out the transits of Jupiter around your chart when they formed trines with its initial position. You are likely to find coincidental positive events initiated by the energy of the giant planet.

Jupiter also produces trines with other elements around the chart. Each one tends to increase the potentials represented by such elements (planets or else) in the areas represented by the Houses concerned.

I have added a list of aphorisms at the end of this chapter to help you analyse Jupiter's transits around a birth chart. They are proposed in two categories, "harmonic" and "dissonant". Do not take them for granted. Use them as guides rather than final products …

THE QUINCUX or INCONJUNCT

The inconjunct aspect is an angle of approximately 150 degrees (150°) between two or more elements around a chart. It represents an ambiguity in the management of the energies involved, with risks of errors due to hesitation or a tendency to let things happen in the hope that possible problems will solve themselves by magic ...

In the same way as the half-sextile and the square, I consider the inconjunct a dissonance because it involves signs belonging to incompatible elements: Fire and Water, Fire and Earth, Air and Water, Air and Earth.

Although these elements coexist on Earth, they do not mix spontaneously like Water and Earth or Air and Fire which form sextiles or oppositions. That is why I do not consider the opposition as dissonant as it is traditionally believed to be. I will explain my point of view later in this chapter.

Jupiter's transit forming an inconjunct with its own position in a chart indicates a period of exaggerated fears and anxiety. Excessive apprehension fluctuates with exuberant enthusiasm, leading to errors and disappointment in the areas represented by Jupiter in the chart.
If it is the ruler of the Ascendant, the effect of Jupiter's transiting inconjunct is more evident in private life. If it rules House II, finances become a source of uncertainty. If it rules House III, it produces doubts and misunderstandings relating to others, or while studying or travelling. The same principle applies for each one of the other Houses.

When Jupiter enters a sign where another planet in discordant aspect with another element in the birth chart, it produces an exaggerated increase of disturbance emanating from what the elements concerned represent (Houses, areas of life, etc.)

In the example chart on the next page, Jupiter transits House III increasing neuronal function (thought-processing and communication) as well as a tendency to aggravate physiological (Chiron) and emotional (Moon) disorders with repercussions in finance management (House VIII) and in the ability to focus on important social or professional projects and ambitions (MC).

This the chart of one of my customers. The question this person asked me was specifically about these areas. Uncertainty increased a reluctance to embark on concrete realization, which is representative of the influence of a transiting inconjunct of Jupiter.

Do not underestimate the role of the inconjunct, too often absent from the analyses of astrologers in their daily practice. The influence of this aspect is such that it can considerably reduce the positive potential of a trine or sextile occurring during the same period ...

In the example chart, Jupiter forms inconjuncts with the Moon in Cancer and a square with Vesta in Virgo that reduce the positive effect of the Moon-Vesta and Moon-Chiron sextiles in the birth chart.

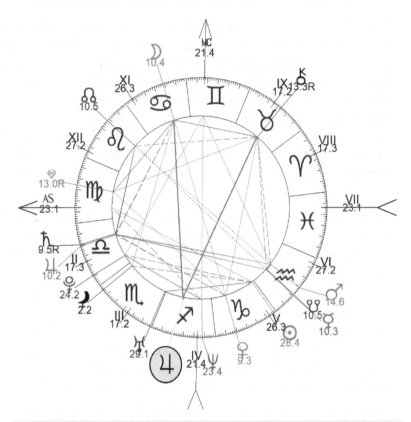

Jupiter transiting in Sagittarius forms an inconjunct with Chiron in Taurus and the Moon in Cancer. Fire sign (Sagittarius) Vs Earth sign (Taurus) and Water sign (Cancer).

When Jupiter forms a transiting inconjunct with an element in the birth chart, errors of appreciation and misjudgement are common.

The effect can last for up to a year, during which a renewed effort is necessary to remain pragmatic and cautious to avoid setbacks and other inconveniences.

Knowing that Jupiter is linked to official matters, the administration, the law, ethics, morals and the philosophical dimension of life, errors and imponderables occurring during this kind of transit are often of an unavoidable nature due to unforeseen events and situations. The inconjunct should therefore be classified as a dissonant aspect. You will find a list of short aphorisms about this type of transiting aspect at the end of this lesson.

THE OPPOSITION

The opposition is an important transit during which all kinds of major events take place. However, it should be noted that in the case of an opposition between a planet in transit and its initial position in the birth chart, a sort of temporary blockage of the energy of this planet is noticed. This phenomenon comes from the fact that the influence of the planet opposing itself is temporally cancelled.

In the case of Jupiter, less enthusiasm and determination may deter the motivation to succeed or progress. Lack of the necessary vigilance to avoid errors of judgment in dealing with official matters is often remarked. The opposition can also produce too much confidence and optimism, too much opportunism, and less moral values. These tendencies undermine objectivity, balance and the happy medium which should instead be chosen when Jupiter is opposed to itself.

This phenomenon is repeated at twelve-year intervals. The first occurs at six years of age, the second at 18, the third at 30, the fourth at 42 and so on until the end of life.

Note that the above ages are not exactly right because Jupiter takes precisely eleven years and three hundred fifteen days to complete a full circle around the zodiac.

Hence, two cycles of Jupiter last for 23 years and 265 days.
Three cycles last for 35 years and 215 days.
Four cycles last for 47 years and 165 days.
Five cycles last for 59 years and one 115 days.
Six cycles last for 71 years and 65 days.
Seven cycles last for 83 years and 15 days.

The transiting conjunctions of faster planets with transiting or natal slower planets make it possible to locate the moments to watch out for. As seen earlier, faster transits act as triggers to events derived from latent tendencies produced by the slower transits.

NOTE: all transiting aspects (except those of the Sun and the Moon) can repeat up to three times. The apparent *retrogradations* are responsible for these phenomena.

The first transiting aspect occurs when the planet moves in *direct motion* around the zodiac.

The second one occurs when the planet, having passed the phase of conjunction or any other aspect, retrogrades and forms the same aspect a few days, weeks, or months later.

The third one occurs when the planet, moving in *direct motion* again, forms the same transiting aspect a third and last time.

A double transiting aspect of Jupiter can extend its influence for up to eight weeks, instead of the three to four weeks of a single transit.

The triple transit, on the other hand, extends Jupiter's activity up to twelve weeks or more.

In fact (and this is an opinion derived from more than four decades in daily practice of astrology), the influence of a planet in a sign is active for the duration of the transit in that sign to a greater or lesser extent until the planet forms an exact conjunction or any other type of aspect with its initial position or with other elements in the chart. The energy of a planet spreads through the sign as soon as it enters it, much like any added substance would modify the molecular structure of water as soon as it is immersed in it.

Memorise this...

Jupiter's retrogradation occurs when it forms the first trine with the Sun. Direct motion resumes four months later, when the Sun forms the second trine with the giant planet.

Here is an example.

Jupiter transits in Sagittarius. The retrograde motion begins when the Sun is in Aries, or about 240° away from Jupiter. This is equivalent to an angle of 120° from Jupiter in Sagittarius to the Sun in Aries. Direct motion resumes when the Sun is in Leo and forms an angle of nearly 120° with Jupiter still in Sagittarius. See the charts below to illustrate this.

11/04/2019 12:00

Therefore, when Jupiter is transiting a certain sign, it is easy to determine the month during which it will start to retrograde and the month when it resumes direct motion.

Because Jupiter's revolution around the Sun is less than twelve years, the moments of retrogradation and direct motion cannot easily be worked out precisely without the ephemeris.

12/08/2019 12:00

In 2007, for example, the retrogradation began on April 6, at 19°47' in Sagittarius. The Sun was at 15°49' in Aries.

In 1995, twelve years earlier, Jupiter in Sagittarius began its retrograde motion on April 2, at 15°43'in the sign. The Sun was at 11°47' in Aries. There was a difference of about 4° to make it a perfect trine of 120°. That year, Jupiter's direct motion resumed on August 3, at 5°32' in Sagittarius, while the Sun was at 10°13' in Leo.

The difference (orb) of 4° mentioned above at the start of the retrograde motion increased by 1° when the planet resumed its direct movement.

A word on the retrogradation phenomenon.

It is an important and often controversial topic in astrology. All kinds of theories are circulating about retrogradation. However, many of us do not really know what it is from an astronomical point of view.

The retrogradation of a planet is an "optical aberration" produced when the Earth on its orbit around the Sun lines up and then overtakes another celestial object (usually a planet or planetoid) always in direct motion on its orbit in such a way that it appears to be moving backwards.

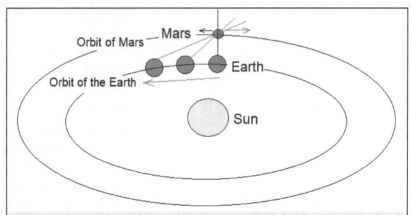

Mars takes twice as long as the Earth to complete a full circle around the Sun. Hence, the Earth overtakes Mars repeatedly every two years or so when the retrogradation phenomenon occurs. From our point of view on Earth, Mars seems to move in reverse.

The optical aberration comes from the apparent fixity of our position on Earth compared to other celestial bodies rotating around the Sun.

That is why it was long believed that the Sun revolved around the Earth which was at the centre of the system...

In reality, the Earth orbits around the Sun at a speed of around 106,000 km/h (~70,000 miles) or almost 30 km/second (20 miles)! In addition, at the equator, the Earth rotates on its axis at 1,700 km/h (about 1,100 miles)! Yet, we do not feel the Earth turning. To us, it is fixed. It therefore seems that everything else in the heavens turn around our planet. This is only true for the Moon …

Even though it is an optical illusion, the physical effect is real. When the Earth overtakes another planet, it moves away from it. The reduction in the radiation of the planet is real. That is why retrogradations must be taken into consideration to fully understand the meaning of a transit.

For example, I usually recommend avoiding any official engagement in anything important during Jupiter's retrograde motion. All kinds of inconveniences can occur in various ways and areas depending on the situation.

I therefore advise my clients to prepare and get organised before Jupiter's retrogradation with the perspective for a concrete and official realization when Jupiter resumes its direct motion.

The retrogradation period can be compared to a gestation phase that lasts until the planet's direct movement resumes. I compare it to baking a cake. Firstly, you prepare the dough (direct movement), secondly you let it rest (retrograde movement) and thirdly, you put it in the oven (resumption of direct movement) to enjoy a result that mainly depends on the quality of the initial procedure.

To conclude this chapter about Jupiter, note that what applies to the transiting aspects of a planet with its initial position in a chart also applies to the transiting aspects with the other elements of the chart.

The harmonious aspects are the sextile and the trine, as well as the conjunction **when it does not amplify a dissonant aspect in the birth chart.**

The dissonant aspects are the square, the inconjunct, and the opposition. In my opinion, you can also include the half-sextile, but it is for you to decide. The conjunction is a discordant aspect when it increases dissonances present in the birth chart.

Remember that Jupiter is essentially a beneficial planet. Its influence is useful to progress in all areas of life. Its transits are even more positive when Jupiter is *strong* in the birth chart. Their effects last for several weeks or even months on either side of the exact aspect. Luck and multiple opportunities are likely to improve life and make it more enjoyable and often richer, materially, socially, intellectually, sentimentally, artistically, or spiritually.

A dissonant transit creates an exaggeration of the tendencies represented by the *radical* planet concerned. The areas represented should be approached with more vigilance. Jupiter can bring good fortune, but it can also cause ruin. Unreasonable optimism and utopian goals are often influenced by dissonant a transit of Jupiter.

Next is a series of aphorisms to help you interpret the transiting aspects of Jupiter with itself and with the other elements of a chart. They are classified into two categories: harmonious aspects and *dissonant aspects*.

THE TRANSITING ASPECTS OF JUPITER

Jupiter in harmony with the Sun

This is announcing a period of increased positive energy, both physically and psychologically. In case of an illness, the condition improves significantly. Jupiter makes any treatment more effective. Optimism and the positive side of the personality are accentuated. The advantage of such harmonious transit in an increase of the potential to progress and succeed in the areas of life represented by Jupiter and the Sun in the birth chart (Houses in Sagittarius and Leo), and by their House positions.

Jupiter in dissonance with the Sun

During such a transit, it is necessary to avoid excesses of any kind and more particularly physically and financially, and in the areas of life represented by the Sun in the birth chart (House in Leo). Too much confidence creates all kinds of errors that are detrimental to the situation. Problems with the law or the administration, or while travelling are frequent during such a transit. Financial losses are often deplored. My advice is to avoid impulsive investments, irresponsible gambling, and stock-market trading. Excessive optimism is frequently responsible for bitter disappointment.

Jupiter in harmony with the Moon

This transit is particularly beneficial to people whose main activity involves significant contact with the public. Artists see their popularity increase during this transit. It frequently produces a significant improvement in social or intimate relationships. The sectors represented by the Moon in the birth chart (House in Cancer) are also boosted. It benefits creation and procreation. This transit of Jupiter also has a beneficial influence on the organisation and evolution of family affairs or residential projects.

Jupiter in dissonance with the Moon

Setbacks are to be expected due to overly optimistic emotional needs and reactions. Problems concerning family members are emerging. In terms of health, all excesses may cause discomfort or illness. Maintaining a balanced diet is essential during this transit. The sectors of life represented by the Moon (House in Cancer) in the birth chart require extra vigilance and care to avoid disappointment resulting from excessive trust and enthusiasm.

Jupiter in harmony with Mercury

Indicates a beneficial period for intellectual work, writing and reading, studies and travels. Sitting at an exam is greatly facilitated during this type of transit. The sectors represented by Mercury in the birth chart (House in Gemini) benefit from temporary improvement with potential long-lasting positive repercussions. This transit improves relationships with siblings and communication skills with their beneficial influence on social, professional, and personal levels.

Jupiter in dissonance with Mercury

More dissonances occurring simultaneously are necessary to forecast real difficulties. Travelling during this time can be a source of setbacks and fatigue. Intellectual work needs extra attention and vigilance to avoid possible errors related to stronger than usual mental energy flow . The sectors represented by Mercury in the birth chart are subject to some degree of aggravation due to excessive optimism, negligence, and errors of judgment.

Jupiter in harmony with Venus

This kind of transit, especially the conjunction, appears to greatly enhance the luck factor with even more intensity if Venus is well aspected in the birth chart, and if it is related to Houses II, V or VIII. The beneficial influence of Jupiter increases personal charm, optimism, and positivity with happy repercussions in most areas of life, particularly those represented by Venus (House in Taurus). Jupiter also enhances artistic creativity and popularity in most Venusian areas of activity.

Jupiter in dissonance with Venus

Other difficult transits are needed to make this one a real problem. However, it usually confers a tendency to overeat and overindulge in earthly pleasures. The attraction to a more expensive way of life may cause memorable setbacks. Jupiter produces errors of judgement in the areas and affairs represented by the House in

Taurus. Sentimental or emotional deception may have a distressing effect and cause exaggerated concern and discontent.

Jupiter in harmony with Mars

This type of transit increases vital energy and improves physiological condition. A more positive approach to life enhances the potential to succeed with significant repercussions in the areas represented by the House in Aries in the birth chart. Jupiter increases courage, combativeness, and efficiency. Diplomacy, patience, and spontaneity are also conferred and are a source of positive motivation for higher levels of achievement.

Jupiter in dissonance with Mars

This transit excessively increases the active principle, which can lead to physiological disorders (increase in blood pressure, nervousness, insomnia, aggressiveness). It produces loss of patience and difficulties to organise activities in an orderly manner. Errors in judgment and mishaps, or accidents, are therefore to be expected if no care is taken to slow down the pace. The sectors represented by the House in Aries need extra attention during such transit.

Jupiter in harmony with Vesta

Such transit improves the ability to harmonise and enhance the potential to succeed in the areas represented by the House in Libra and the House where it is found in the birth chart. More openness and goodwill can solve all kinds of problems and restore or preserve peace and well-being. A positive effect on fertility and productivity or creativity is also noted with happy repercussions in the areas related to Vesta strongly favoured by the energy of Jupiter.

Jupiter in dissonance with Vesta

The search for the good or the better things of life becomes less rational. Errors in judgment and operation result from lack of concentration. Opportunism is more noticeable. Being too optimistic and too confident make speculation rather dubious and a source of financial loss. The desire for success is strong, but courage changed into temerity shows potential detrimental consequences. Moral or ethical values should prevail to avoid mishaps during this transit.

Jupiter in harmony with itself

Such transit corresponds to a period of general improvement. There is a feeling of being "protected by the gods", able to turn lead into gold ... If Jupiter is well aspected and strong in the birth chart, a very prosperous period is predictable when social or financial situation improves significantly. Travel abroad, investments and speculation, studies and relationships with important people are likely to provide more satisfaction and success. This transit is particularly remarkable during the periods of direct motion of the planet.

Jupiter in dissonance with itself

This transit is likely to produce an irrational increase in optimism and trust in oneself and others. There will be moments of unhappiness due a tendency to exaggerate the importance of problems. Speculation is not recommended. Lack of objectivity, and excessive opportunism hinder objectivity and the potential to succeed. Irresponsible spending, gambling or stock market losses, and risky investments are often deplored during a dissonant transiting aspect of Jupiter with its natal position. The sectors of life linked to the House in Sagittarius are more likely to be affected.

Jupiter in harmony with Saturn

This transit promotes a more significant ability to pursue daily activities successfully. This is particularly so in the areas of life represented by the Houses ruled by Jupiter and Saturn in the birth chart. Jupiter allows a clearer appreciation of life, a more open and determined mindset to deal with projects, situations, and problems more effectively. Passed experience confers a rational approach to situations and promotes advancement and concrete realisation.

Jupiter in dissonance with Saturn

The whole chart must be analysed to determine the strength of this transit. If a dissonance exists in the natal chart between Jupiter and Saturn, this period must be considered with the greatest prudence. Various problems are to be expected, mainly in the sectors represented by Jupiter and Saturn in the birth chart. Mishaps are often due to an overabundance of optimism or, on the contrary, of _apathy and negative carelessness. If Saturn is strong in the chart and well aspected, Jupiter does not have such a strong influence, unless other transits accentuate this transiting dissonance._

Jupiter in harmony with Chiron

This type of transit tends to improve health condition because it increases the ability to analyse the different causes for potential disorders to prevent or cure them. Jupiter also favours evolution in the areas represented by Chiron in the birth chart (the House in Virgo and the House where it is positioned). A more rational approach to life's situations improves their significance and potentials.

Jupiter in dissonance with Chiron

During this transit, health is likely to become a growing source of concern. There may be a tendency to exaggerate that may worsen or accentuate unpleasant symptoms. The effect of Jupiter highlights realities that do not necessarily deserve as much emphasis. After all, the human machine is not so wonderful as we are led to believe! However, the more we focus on what is wrong, the more we forget what is doing well. Hypochondriacs become particularly intense during this kind of transit ... Note that the conjunction also tends to produce a similar undesirable effect ...

Jupiter in harmony with Uranus

This type of transit is excellent for the nervous system and psychological balance. It accentuates optimism and adaptability. There is a stronger need to socialise, with happy repercussions in the areas represented by Uranus in the birth chart (House in Aquarius). Improvements are to be expected because Jupiter helps carry out innovating projects successfully. Jupiter and Uranus may also increase the luck factor, particularly favouring gamblers, artists, and adventurers or inventors. Unexpected opportunities can lead to very positive changes in life during such a transit.

Jupiter in dissonance with Uranus

During this transit, projects are rather extravagant. Serious losses due to mismanagement or to a wrong appreciation of reality are to be expected. The desire to change is confronted to unexpected events *that can produce difficult social and financial situations. The sectors represented by Uranus in the birth chart are primarily concerned. To keep on the safe side, it is better to postpone important projects to avoid the risk of unpleasant and costly outcomes.*

Jupiter in harmony with Neptune
This type of transit favours artists and people involved in mystical, religious, or occult activities. It also seems to have a positive influence to help cure or control physiological and psychological disorders. Jupiter has a strong influence on imagination, and it increases creativity in the areas represented by the House in Pisces. More intuition and a better connection with the spiritual dimension of life favours beneficial situations that are perceived and dealt with more philosophically.

Jupiter in dissonance with Neptune
A tendency to give too much credit to unrealistic schemes increases the risk of costly disappointment. This type of transit causes a certain weariness of both body and soul. Self-indulgence leads to excessive lack of rigor and self-control. Illnesses are likely to worsen because treatments seem less effective. Allergic reactions to medicine are possible. This kind of transit is a source of concern for people with glandular, hormonal, respiratory, endocrinal, or psychological conditions.

Jupiter in harmony with Pluto
Such transit promotes physiological and psychological regeneration that allows quick recovery from all kinds of ailments. This type of transit is also good for concentration and patience. It becomes possible to take on daunting tasks with a degree of optimism that enables to overcome most obstacles with ease. This is a period when inner strength is a profound source of satisfaction, achievement, and success in the areas represented by both planets in the birth chart (Houses in Sagittarius and Scorpio).

Jupiter in dissonance with Pluto
There is always some tension during such a transit that produces a tendency to lose patience and feel oppressed and obsessed by

negative elements. It is strongly advised to control personal desires in the areas represented by Pluto to avoid mistakes and problems that may have an official or legal connotation. Excessive sexual needs are often influenced by this type of transit. Appropriate dietary habits and hygiene are to be observed.

Jupiter in harmony with the Ascendant
This type of transit promotes inner feelings, and latent potentials. It enhances charisma and charm and favours a kinder approach to private matters and relationships. Producing simultaneously a positive aspect with the Descendant (House VII) Jupiter may favour an important contract or partnership and positive motivation that may perdure for a whole year. The benefit often comes from the areas of life represented by Jupiter in the chart (House in Sagittarius).

Jupiter in dissonance with the Ascendant
This a period of excessive accentuation of the inner self tempered by other values stemming from the areas represented by Jupiter in the birth chart (House in Sagittarius and House where Jupiter is). Depending on the aspect (square or opposition) family affairs (House IV), social status (House X) or marriage and other important partnerships may become a source of over excitement due to major social, professional, or familial projects, to the detriment of more profound personal needs.

Jupiter in harmony with the MidHeaven
This type of transit usually corresponds to a period of significant social or professional evolution. Career advancement or promotion, substantial progression of important projects, obtention of diplomas, certifications and other gratifying rewards are greatly favoured. The positive influence of Jupiter stems from the areas represented by this planet in the chart (House in Sagittarius and House where Jupiter transits).

Jupiter in dissonance with the MidHeaven
A tendency to aim too high may produce unwise investments, financially or otherwise. Being over positive and ambitious renders less objective, therefore more vulnerable to misjudgement and their

disagreeable consequences. The areas represented by Jupiter in the chart (House in Sagittarius) need to be seriously taken into consideration to control imprudent engagements that would affect the areas represented by the House where Jupiter transits. Remember that Jupiter represents the law, regulations, and the administration...

There is nothing definitive in these short interpretations. The same rule applies to all the other aphorisms in this book. They are written only to guide your own interpretations, not to force a conclusion. Let yourself be inspired by your intuition and philosophy of life, rather than by a few written words which are only humble examples of what can be said of the various types of transits of Jupiter in aspect with the other elements in the chart.

Lesson 3

SATURN

The concept of limitation is represented by Saturn. This planet is associated with the lessons of life, obstacles, and karmic tests necessary to become stronger, more responsible, more confident, and more aware of the realities and responsibilities of life.

With Saturn, difficulties become a remedy for weakness, as the struggle required to deal with them strengthens latent potentials that gradually lead to self-realisation and wisdom. This journey may require several incarnations. The notion of karma related to Saturn, allows self-criticism to make the necessary adjustments until the last moments of life, when the time has come to prepare for the next one ...

Saturn takes twenty-nine and a half years to circle around the zodiac. It would take an entire book to explain the influence of Saturn, so important at all levels. Read my "Astrology for a better life" book to learn more about Saturn. However, beyond anything you will find in astrology literature, your own practice is the best way to perfect your knowledge of the natal and transiting influences of Saturn.

Before you analyse the possible effects of its transits, you must take note of its role in the birth chart.

If Saturn is "strong" in a birth chart, its transits also have a strong influence and they usually coincide with milestone events.

When Saturn is "weak" in a birth chart, it often confers a fatalistic approach to life's events rather than the will to actively deal with them. To consider oneself a "victim" weakens the potential to learn from difficulties. In that case, Saturn's transits are considered negatively rather than as an opportunity to progress by learning from life's numerous challenges.

Strong Saturn and weak Saturn...

1 - Strong Saturn

- First and foremost, any planet is strong when it is positioned in its sign of rulership. In Saturn's case: Capricorn.
- Saturn is strong in House X, symbolically connected to the tenth sign, Capricorn.
- Saturn is also strong when it is in House I (the Ascendant) or in the other two angular Houses (IV and VII).
- Saturn is also strong when it is in conjunction with the Sun, the Moon, the ruler of the Ascendant or the ruler of the Midheaven (MC).
- Saturn is strong when it is involved in many aspects or in aspect (harmonic or dissonant) with the ruler of the Ascendant, the cusp of the Ascendant, or the Midheaven, and with the Sun or the Moon.
- Finally, Saturn is strong when it is dominant in the chart, according to my method of the planetary chains explained in my "Astrology for a better life" and "Horary Astrology" books available from the Amazon website in your region or from your local bookstore.

2 - Weak Saturn

- They say Saturn is weak when it is in its sign of exile or fall, but I disagree with this theory.
- Saturn is in fact never really or totally "weak". Its influence is only less perceived, less active, depending on what extent the planet is involved in aspects with other elements in the birth chart.
- When no major aspects involve Saturn, it seems that its influence is weaker, but it is nonetheless operational in the House where it is found in relation with the House it rules (House in Capricorn).
- The influence of Saturn can be weakened by harmonic aspects that can dilute its natural "karmic" influence.

The table on the next page summarizes the moments of life when Saturn forms major aspects with its own position in the birth chart.

Saturn in aspect with its own position at birth				
Sextile	Square	Trine	Opposition	Inconjunct
Age	Age	Age	Age	Age
5	7	10	14 - 15	12
24	21	19	43 - 44	17
33-34	36	39	72 - 73	42
53	51	48	101 - 102	47
63	65	68		71
82	80	77		76

Only three conjunctions are possible: at 29/30, at 58/59, at 87/88

The ages above are approximate. Always check the ephemeris to make sure you are analysing the right configuration.

THE CONJUNCTION

During a lifetime, three conjunctions of transiting Saturn with its own position at birth are possible. The first takes place at 29 and a half years of age, the second at around 58/59 and the third one at around 87/88. Few humans experience a fourth one, at around 117 ...

The return of Saturn signals the end of a cycle and the start of a new one. Its meaning is different from the previous one although it greatly depends on it in various ways.

The first cycle of Saturn, from birth to the thirtieth year, is what I call the *acquiring cycle of life*. During this period, one learns to speak, read, write, count and to do many other things that will be useful during the second cycle.

The second cycle of Saturn lasts until the age of 59. It is what I call, the *building cycle of life*. During this period of almost thirty years, we strive to realize ourselves concretely. We assume all kinds of realities and responsibilities; we realise many projects ... In other words, we try to take our place in the world as concretely and durably as possible.

The quality of this second cycle of Saturn depends on the previous one, but there are times when we take our distances from what we learned during the first cycle. We are more mature when Saturn returns to its original position. Life and the perception of the future take on another form.

The three decades that constitute the second cycle are very important because they lead to the second return of Saturn to its initial position when the third cycle is about to begin ...

The third cycle of Saturn takes us into old age. This is what I call *the harvesting cycle*. Saturn's second return to its original position occurs between the ages of 58 and 60, when most of us prepare for retirement, for *harvesting time*. Abundance during this third cycle naturally depends on what we have done during the second cycle ...

This third cycle opens new horizons. Retirement makes it possible to appreciate life differently. The reward is proportional to what has been accomplished in three decades. Freed from daily constraints retirement life allows for new projects, new aspirations, new horizons. Many people simply savour their freedom spontaneously. Although different from one person to another, the entry into the third cycle of Saturn remains a decisive event in many ways.

The fourth cycle of Saturn begins at around 87. Those who reach this noble age understand that they are on the "last stretch" of their life. Knowing that Pluto transits opposite its initial position in the chart, the end of life becomes more concrete and above all, inevitable ... That is probably why the body and the mind tend to slow down. Time takes on a different meaning. Hours and days seem longer. The slower the better to postpone the last moment of life awaited with wisdom, calm, and honorable resignation ...

Saturn and the other elements of the chart

Contrary to what is usually believed, when transiting Saturn creates a conjunction with another planet or element around the chart, rather than blocking its function, my experience shows that it allows concrete realisation of the latent influence represented by the planet or element in question.

The duration of a transiting conjunction of Saturn varies from a few weeks to several months depending on the retrogradation periods previously mentioned in the lesson about Jupiter. Up to three occurrences are possible; the first when Saturn is in direct motion (D), the second when it is in retrograde mode (R) and the third after the planet resumes its direct motion (D).

The Saturnian taboos ...

For many beginners and experienced astrologers alike, the arrival of Saturn on a sensitive point of a birth chart is too often considered negatively. *Saturn has a bad reputation!* This is so perhaps because it represents the efforts necessary to overcome obstacles, limitations, and difficulties before reaching the coveted goals ...

However, I have noticed that a transiting conjunction of Saturn often coincides with a major achievement in the areas represented by the planet or element concerned.

The conjunction between transiting Saturn and an element of a chart occurs only once in thirty years or so. Its rarity contributes to the importance of the event that usually implies long-lasting repercussions. Such event should therefore not be overlooked or minimized.

Saturn forces us to recognise what must be done concretely and properly to face up to our responsibilities. The next conjunction occurring nearly thirty years later represents a potential payback for the efforts and the work done during the preceding period of almost thirty years.

A transit of Saturn always returns something that dates back to the previous conjunction. Knowing this for a fact helps understand the influence of the transit to deal with it in a more constructive manner.

THE HALF-SEXTILE

Two 30° aspects of Saturn with its original position in the chart occur during its complete revolution around the zodiac. They have two different meanings.

The first one follows is also the first aspect Saturn creates with itself after birth. The child is between two-and-a-half and five years old. It is a period of discovery of the world around. The body and the intellect are growing fast. The first restrictions are imposed by the carers (parents or other people). Learning is at a cost. Falls and other errors can be painful. This is the first period of maturation, when the child learns to control the natural functions.

The second half-sextile occurs approximately between the ages of 26 and 28/29, before the return of Saturn around its original sign-position. Much has been learned since the first half-sextile. The experience acquired triggers many questions about personal ambitions, projects, career, and other crucial objectives. Doubt feeds or deter motivation, depending on how the passed 25 years or so have been led. It is time to prepare for the return of Saturn, when what is obtained is directly linked to the amount of work, effort, and determination involved in the pursuit of life's higher goals.

THE SEXTILE

Two sextiles with its initial position occur during a complete revolution of Saturn around the zodiac. See the list at the beginning of this lesson if your need to refresh your memory.

Each of these periods is marked by improved awareness. The first occurs around the age of 5, when the child moves from kindergarten to primary school. The second sextile forms around the age of 24, a time of more concrete social, personal, or professional accomplishment. Simultaneously, Jupiter makes the second return to its original position in the chart.

When the third sextile occurs, at 33 or 34 years of age, the construction cycle mentioned above takes on its full value. More important projects are emerging and organised.

The fourth sextile occurs at 53, an important moment often marked by major events related to aspirations and potentials in accordance with the efforts made to maintain and consolidate personal and social status.

Regardless of the age, when it occurs the sextile of Saturn with its initial position represents a moment of affirmation and progression towards the goals that have been set.

While the conjunction is surely the most remarkable transiting aspect, the others should not be neglected. The sextile is one of them.

A transiting sextile of Saturn with any other element of the chart increases the ability to manage such element and the area (House) it represents.

Note that the sextile represents a "potential" that needs to be taken advantage of to derive concrete positive results in the areas concerned. Otherwise, nothing more than a slight improvement with no significant consequences would ensue.

THE SQUARE

The periods during which Saturn forms a square with its own position are often uncomfortable and unpleasant. There is a feeling of being somehow diminished, limited, slowed down, and discouraged. However, the efforts made are useful to derive more concrete results during the following transits: the sextile or the trine.

The first square.

The first square occurs during childhood, around the age of 7 or 8. At this young age, the realities of life are mainly derived from education and the constraints that come with it. For many youngsters it is difficult to integrate into the social group at school and at home. When health problems occur, they are often the results of inner frustrations which causes stem from the transition between being a toddler and a child. Elementary schooling started a couple of years earlier, but now its role is more serious and real. The responsibilities of life become a daily challenging task ...

The second square

There was a time when adulthood was officialised at 21. I remember in the seventies in Australia, I had a big party on my 21st birthday to celebrate this major milestone. A key was usually offered, in various forms (greeting cards, for example) as a symbol of coming of age supposed to give access to the rights and "privileges" that adulthood has to offers.

At the same time, the many responsibilities of adulthood came true. The right to move out from the family home and find a "better place" to live; the right to vote and to decide on the country's political future; the right to do all those things that were not accessible to children and teenagers ...

Although often impatiently awaited, adulthood also corresponds to the start on a hazardous path. Becoming an adult also means being legally responsible for one's actions. Unable to manage themselves responsibly, influenced by their entourage and an inexperienced philosophy of life, many have discovered to their expense the high cost of growing up.

However, this major passport to adulthood makes it possible to assert oneself and to begin building a future despite a horizon that may seem bleak and uninviting, even threatening, and not really encouraging ...

The third square

The third square occurs around the age of 36. The weight of responsibilities has increased since the second quadrature. Often, marriage and children have changed daily life radically. For some, the first grey hairs appear. Many men are going slightly bald. More burdens mean more worries, at work and at home. Time has a more concrete influence on the perception of the future. Nostalgia is triggered by reminiscent flashbacks and the first thoughts about the "good old days"...

Although a little dull and austere for some of us, such a period is useful because it motivates us to improve the potential to progress on the social and professional ladder. The future is perceived in a more realistic manner. Financial and personal investments are considered more seriously.

The fourth transiting square occurs at about 51, together with the return of Chiron on its original position. The fifth one is active at around 65, and the sixth one at 80. If you live much older, the seventh square will be a source of concern when you are around 95 years old.

About these transiting squares of Saturn with its original position, common sense should be sufficient to understand how they may influence life. If you have already lived through a few transiting squares, remember what happened and how you felt during the previous one. It will be useful to understand what the next one may produce.

The transiting squares of Saturn with the other elements of the chart tend to lessen the potential and motivation in the areas represented by the elements concerned (the Houses ruled by such element).

You will find a list of aphorisms to help you analyse harmonious and dissonant transiting aspects of Saturn with major elements around a birth chart.

THE TRINE

The first transiting trine of Saturn with its original position occurs at 10 or 11 years of age. The time has come to enter secondary school. Most children ignore what they want to do with their life, but they are both proud and a little anxious to step into the older student's group. Of course, such important evolution depends on the child's overall results in primary studies, made more difficult during the previous transiting square period mentioned earlier in this lesson.

The second trine occurs at around 19 or 20, when the young person is about to take off as an adult to realise personal ambitions and a successful career. For many, those are the college years, when their future is being built and organised. The motivation is strong and usually backed by good results, coinciding with the positive effect of the trine.

The third transiting trine occurs at 39 or 40. Passed experiences are numerous. Marriage, children, a steady job, and other developments have made it possible to climb up the social ladder. Some succeed more than others of course, but overall, this third trine corresponds to a two-year period marked by a degree of improvement that depends on many factors in the birth chart, other planetary transits and personal drive, willpower, and motivation.

This second trine follows the third transiting square mentioned earlier in this lesson. It is and interesting period during which the lessons learned from the preceding two-and-half-year transiting square become a source of renewed motivation and concrete realisation.

The fourth trine occurs at 48 or 49, the fifth one between 68 and 69, and the sixth one at 77 or 78 years of age. A seventh one is possible at around 98 years of age …

Each transiting trine formed by Saturn with its own position or the positions of other elements in the chart corresponds to a time of affirmation and increase of the potential to realise important projects, depending on the amount of work and effort produced to succeed.

Saturn is not associated with what we get for free, like presents or unexpected opportunities. On the contrary, Saturn symbolises the logical path from cause to effect. We receive only what we deserve, nothing more, nothing less. Wise investments get positive returns, while imprudent budgeting leads to economic failure. While everyone makes mistakes, from the ability to recognise our flaws, useful lessons are learned and applied to feed personal experience and the potential for longer-lasting success.

The areas most concerned by the transits of Saturn are those it represents in the chart (House in Capricorn), those belonging to the House in which it is found, and to the House where Saturn transits. The same rule applies to all other transits.

Remember that a transiting aspect can form at the same time as another of different nature. Trines and squares from different sources are often occurring simultaneously. They require more attention to determine the true value of such contradicting influences.

In the example chart on the next page, the tendency to indulge in various excesses due to the transiting square formed by Jupiter with its radical position, is reduced by the transiting trine formed by Saturn with its radical position. However, in this chart, transiting Jupiter is forming a square with radical Saturn, while transiting Saturn forms a sextile with radical Jupiter. These configurations can be said to collaborate and complement one another, while combating one another to the point of annihilation.

Those transits may finally bring nothing more than a neutral result with no remarkable returns in the areas represented by the Houses concerned. Configurations with other elements, such as the Sun, the Moon, the ruler of the Ascendant, the MC or any other important element in the chart may bring more concrete satisfaction and positive results.

In the example chart below, transiting Jupiter in Sagittarius forms a square with its own position in Pisces, while transiting Saturn in Capricorn forms a trine with its own position in Virgo. There are many more transiting aspects formed by Jupiter and Saturn in transit with many other elements in the chart. Can you see them?

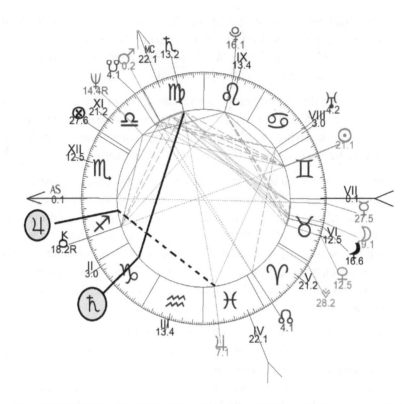

THE INCONJUNCT

The periods during which transiting Saturn forms an inconjunct with its own position are marked by a tendency to wonder why things are not moving as fast as expected and why the results are disappointing in comparison with the effort and work done.

The inconjunct brings forward what needs to be done concretely, but it does not confer the spontaneous will to get to work. To wait until later is a major source of stagnation that considerably slows down the process of concrete realisation. This type of transit can also coincide with health concerns and their detrimental impact on physical and psychological potentials necessary to keep up the pace to reach important objectives or realise major projects.

There are two types of inconjuncts. One follows the trine, while the other follows the opposition. Their roles are different.

The first one corresponds to a period of self-satisfaction issued from the success promoted by the preceding transiting trine. In that case, it is possible to take a rest or to delegate some of the workload, thanks to the good results obtained during the previous period. Such approach may be useful to prepare for the transiting opposition that follows the inconjunct.

The second one corresponds to a period of relative laziness succeeding to many months when transiting Saturn was in opposition with its own position in the chart. The important events and challenging situations thus produced had to be dealt with in an orderly manner to take advantage of the opposition.

During the transiting inconjunct, vigilance is required to avoid errors stemming from a tendency to let go rather than to be on the go as needed.

Note that the following transiting aspect being a trine, it seems important to prepare for it actively during the inconjunct period. Remember that the benefit of a transiting trine of Saturn is proportional to the investment in terms of work, effort, endurance, and determination.

THE OPPOSITION

The first opposition between transiting Saturn and its radical position occurs around the age of 15, when teenagers strive to free themselves from the restricting authority of their parents and educators. Not children anymore, but not adults, adolescents navigate in an uncomfortable no man's land zone.

The need to impose personal needs and evacuate frustrations is linked to the effect of this major transit. Saturn opposes itself, cancelling its restricting influence long enough for youngsters to revendicate their rights and their freedom.

The fifteen-year-old's emancipation stems from a strong need to express personal opinions and preferences in an often clumsy but genuine manner. However, the complexity of this period is necessary to prepare for adulthood. From the transit of Saturn in opposition with itself emanates a spontaneous yearning to oppose others to test personal limits and to reveal inner needs and talents more concretely.

The second opposition occurs at around 43 or 44 years of age, during the same period as transiting Uranus in opposition with itself. The transits of Uranus will be treated later in this book.

It is an immensely important period when unexpected radical changes are likely. The weight of the responsibilities dealt with since the first return of Saturn explained earlier, becomes too heavy to carry. An intense and sometimes unconscious need for freedom, motivates major movements in predominant areas of life. Some, more adventurous, agree to drastic modifications of their future and take irreversible decisions. Others do their upmost to preserve the status quo despite the inner turmoil. The karmic nature of Saturn puts all sentient beings to the test of earthly time…

The third transiting opposition of Saturn with its own position in the chart occurs at 73 or 74 years of age. This is a critical time, when a form of liberation is put forward by important events and the need to preserve what has been earned and learned since the previous transiting opposition, thirty years earlier. Health has become a more important topic; to preserve or restore it is now a vital necessity.

This third transiting opposition produces a release of energy that can either favour evolution or increase difficulties. More fragile than thirty years earlier, both body and mind are not as strong and motivated to continue the fight for a better life. Old age is showing although most people in their seventies today are in good shape, thanks to a wiser approach to their health condition and to the progress of medicine.

Because a fourth transiting opposition is most unlikely, this one creates a need to make the best of the few decades left to enjoy life.

Memories help keep up the pace to enjoy the present moment and immediate future more completely.

Saturn and the other elements in the chart

The aspect works differently when Saturn forms a transiting opposition with another element in the chart. Beyond the usual diminution of the energy in the areas represented by the element and House concerned, this type of configuration has an undeniable karmic meaning.

As explained in the previous chapter, the opposition involves compatible and complementary signs: Air and Fire, Water and Earth. However, in the case of an opposition such complementarity is less flagrant than a sextile.

We can compare the opposition to what happens in a democratic government. Although opposed in their opinions, political parties complement one another. They allow laws to be more equitable and fairer for everyone.

The opposition between transiting Saturn and a planet or other element in the chart corresponds to a challenging period during which the efforts and work done increase the potential to deal with the realities of life in a more mature and efficient manner.

A transit never acts alone.

It is necessary to take other transiting influences into account during the transit of the planet you are looking at. For example, in 2016 Jupiter was transiting in Virgo, while Saturn was in Sagittarius since 2015. There was a transiting square between the two giant planets. The aspect reduced the energy of Jupiter which, in turn, enhanced Saturn's. At the same time, Neptune transiting in Pisces made an opposition with Jupiter and a square with Saturn…

Mixed dissonances need to be analysed carefully to determine precisely what they may produce during the period concerned. In 2016, the positive energy stemming from a trine between transiting Pluto in Capricorn with Jupiter in Virgo backed by a transiting sextile between Neptune and Pluto bring more major combinations to analyse before making any definite prognosis or forecast.

Example

For a Taurus or Capricorn person, Jupiter had a positive influence in terms of evolution, progress, and success. However, due to the transiting square formed with Saturn, Jupiter's influence was not as strong, while Saturn's effect was amplified by the transiting square with Jupiter. In addition, the influence of Neptune in discordance with Saturn produced interferences between dreams (Neptune) and reality (Saturn). Meanwhile, Pluto's role was quite useful as it conferred more resilience and perseverance to deal with difficulties and limitations more effectively.

As already mentioned, Saturn does not have a very good reputation. It is not considered a beneficial planet. Saturn is "Cronos", the god of time. The effect of time is easily verified, both physically and mentally. Time affects everything. Time acts on brain cells (neurons) and on our cognitive faculties. It plays a role in the initial process of cellular growth and later deterioration. It also favours the evolution of our intellect and general mental and physical capacities.

Before the discoveries of Uranus, Neptune and Pluto, Saturn was associated with death. Nowadays, Pluto, the "god of death and guardian of hell" has earned this meaning. Saturn is now linked to old age and wisdom issued from life's events and time.

Saturn represents experience and knowledge acquired while dealing with hardships and the lessons they teach to make us more resistant and self-confident in the presence of difficulties. Success requires much effort and work, sacrifices, patience, and determination. A beneficial transit of Saturn enhances the natural potential to improve durably in the areas represented by this planet (House in Capricorn) and by the other elements concerned. A discordant transit puts pressure and increases limitations and difficulties. The action needed to surmount life's obstacles improves personal performances.

When Saturn is well aspected in a birth chart, its discordant transits are usually less distressing or detrimental. Other simultaneous discordant transits are necessary to enhance the damaging effect of Saturn.

The influence of transiting Saturn lasts many months to more than a year depending on retrogradations.

My research has shown that the effect of a conjunction between transiting Saturn and radical Saturn every twenty-nine and a half years, begins as soon as Saturn enters the sign where it was at birth. Taking one year into consideration seems sufficient, but I have seen numerous cases where the influence of Saturn lasted for the duration of the transit through a complete sign: two and a half years.

Sensibility to the movements of Saturn depends on its natal position and to the aspects it forms with important elements of the birth chart, together with its hierarchical status (dominant). The effect of a transiting conjunction is operational long before the exact aspect. The entry of Saturn in a sign immediately sends a strong message to whatever is in that sign. Saturn imposes itself in a very demanding and compelling manner.

In conclusion, concerning a transit of Saturn there is an undeniable responsibility to remain vigilant and prudent in the process of analysing its possible influence. It must be observed in accordance with the rest of the chart, despite its obvious role often remarkably independent of all other astrological aspects.

In the following pages you will find a series of aphorisms designed to help you analyse the transits of Saturn in relation to itself and to the other elements of the birth chart. They are listed in two groups: harmonious and *dissonant* transiting aspects.

THE TRANSITING ASPECTS OF SATURN

Saturn in harmony with the Sun

This transit accentuates the drive and motivation to make concrete realisations. Saturn improves patience and efficiency. Personal opinions are more stable and credible. In case of a conjunction, there may be loss of vital energy, but this transit also indicates a period of important realisation that depends on the work done during the years before this transit of Saturn. The radical aspects involving the Sun in the birth chart must be taken into consideration to evaluate more precisely the incidence of this transit.

Saturn in dissonance with the Sun

This transit tends to restrict the ability to act by lowering both the physical and psychological energy flows. The areas represented by the Sun (House in Leo and House where the Sun is) are mostly concerned and may be tempered by delays and other unpleasant situations. Fatigue and loss of motivation may need to be treated with food supplements rich in vitamins, oligo elements and minerals. Skin, joints and bones are often a source of discomfort or pain during such a transit of Saturn that can last for many months.

Saturn in harmony with the Moon

Saturn has a beneficial influence on the expression and handling of emotions. Natural creativity is enhanced with potentially good concrete results that may have long-lasting repercussions. The areas represented by the Moon (House in Cancer and House where the Moon is) may greatly benefit from this kind of transit that can last many months. Family affairs and place of residence are also concerned and should benefit from the strong influence of Saturn.

Saturn in dissonance with the Moon

This transit tends to have a physiological effect with psychological consequences. The hormonal and lymphatic functions are troubled by the restrictive influence of Saturn. Emotional loss of reactivity may hide a depression. A lighter view of life must be preferred to melancholy and introversion. An effort is needed to deal with difficulties of karmic nature that may linger on for many months. The areas represented by the Moon (House in Cancer and House where the Moon is) are more concerned by a slower than usual activity.

Saturn in harmony with Mercury

This type of transit increases mental assimilation and intellectual maturity. Favourable during studies, Saturn improves memory and comprehension. Interesting and valuable lessons are learnt by sharing thoughts and ideas with elders or more experienced people. Travelling is also a source of concrete and long-lasting satisfactions. Saturn is beneficial to all subjects and projects depending on the ability to communicate, to share thoughts and ideas, as well as the motivation to progress in the areas represented by Mercury in the birth chart (House in Gemini and House where Mercury is).

Saturn in dissonance with Mercury

A loss of performance in communication due to loss of motivation and some difficulty to activate mental processes are consequent to this type of transit. Saturn puts pressure by imposing constraints that require much effort for little result. Fate may also play a discordant role by ways of delays, travel setbacks, failures at exams, and other situations produced by poorer cerebral efficiency. Saturn tends to weaken neuronal activity, increasing loss of memory and other nuisances which may be preventable by daily physical exercise and by adding vitamins in diet.

Saturn in harmony with Venus

Beneficial to artists, due to the increase in the ability to harmonise and create, this type of transit is, however, useful to everyone. It favours long-term romantic commitments. It increases fertility and confers a more rational and mature approach to the good things of life. It reduces the tendency to various excesses, both sensual and sentimental, and improves determination, patience, and compassion to deal with the realities of life in the areas represented by the Houses in Taurus and Capricorn, and the House where Saturn transits.

Saturn in dissonance with Venus

This type of transit tends to weaken fertility and creativity. It may produce a long period of partial or complete loss of inspiration with detrimental effects in artistic careers or family projects. Less interest in expressing love means less enjoyment and less success in romantic pursuits. The areas of life represented by Venus (House in Taurus and House where Venus is) are primarily concerned. Healthwise, Saturn may impact thyroid function or create gynaecological discomfort. Loss of sexual appetite is also derived from a dissonant aspect between transiting Saturn and natal Venus.

Saturn in harmony with Mars

During this type of transit, the ability to act and react is enhanced and made more constructive with superior results and long-lasting realisations. Improved coordination makes for better decisions and quicker reactions. Efficiency is enhanced at work and in sporting activities. Feeling stronger and calmer increases self-confidence and the ability to win. The areas represented by Mars (House in Aries and House where natal mars is found) are mostly credited by this beneficial transit that lasts for many months.

Saturn in dissonance with Mars

This type of transit is like applying the brake in a car while pressing on the accelerator pedal. The engine raves up, but the wheels cannot turn. The result is a noisy standstill that can damage the vehicle. Frustration emanates from such a transit. Personal physical performances are affected. Less motivation and more fatigue reduce the potential to win and even the drive to reach the finish line. Healthwise, Saturn seems to lower physical resistance. Iron and vitamin C intakes may counteract tiredness and general loss of energy. The areas of life represented by Mars (House in Aries and House where natal Mars is found) are primarily concerned.

Saturn in harmony with Vesta

This transit represents a period of harmonisation and stabilisation in the areas represented by Vesta (House in Libra and House where natal Vesta is found) with potentially long-lasting repercussions. The ability to handle daily affairs with more diplomacy and patience improves the quality of relationships and their positive influence in various ways. Important partnerships and contracts are likely, depending on personal needs and aspirations.

Saturn in dissonance with Vesta

This period is marked by more responsibilities to tackle while making every possible effort to preserve balance and harmony in the areas represented by Vesta (House in Libra and House where natal Vesta is found). Setbacks are likely in personal relationships or professional partnerships. Fate may also play a role by postponing or slowing down the realisation of important projects, or by increasing the amount of paperwork or requests from the administration or other official sources.

Saturn in harmony with Jupiter

This is a constructive transit, a period during which personal ambitions and opportunities combined may strongly favour concrete and durable evolution. This likely to be more remarkable in the areas of life represented by Jupiter (House in Sagittarius and House where natal Jupiter is found). While it lasts, the positive influence of Saturn should coincide with satisfying results following a long period of work and effort when Saturn was transiting in dissonance with Jupiter, prior to this harmonious transit.

Saturn in dissonance with Jupiter

During this long period, Saturn reduces enthusiasm and enterprising spirit because of situations and events that may discourage the desire to succeed. Things are not going as planned. Frustration emanates from a feeling that so much must be done to obtain so little. However, the restricting influence of Saturn is useful because challenges and obstacles are meant to be overcome to test endurance and determination by accepting that time is the key to long-lasting realisation. This will particularly apply to the areas represented by Jupiter in the chart (House in Sagittarius and House where natal Jupiter is found).

Saturn in harmony with itself

This transit corresponds to a period of affirmation of the self and confirmation in the areas represented by Saturn in the chart (House in Capricorn and House where natal Saturn is found). While it lasts (up to two and half years) the latent influence of Saturn is enriched in a positive manner. Thus, discordant aspects involving Saturn in the birth chart seize to be a source of blockage, delays, and setbacks. On the contrary, they trigger and facilitate evolution and success. However, with Saturn the degree of realisation depends on the effort and work done to overcome past difficulties.

Saturn in dissonance with itself
Whereas the opposition would tend to lift the eventual restrictions represented by Saturn in the chart, the square and the inconjunct seem more prejudicial to the ability and will to obtain the results expected from the amount of work done. Much effort for little gratification is often remarked during this type of transit. Because it can last up to two and half years, it may become less apparent as time goes by. The areas represented by Saturn (House in Capricorn, House where natal Saturn is found, and House where Saturn transits) are likely to be a source of frustration and unsatisfaction. However, efforts made during this period will be rewarded when Saturn transits in harmony with its own position.

Saturn in harmony with Chiron
This type of transit is a source of physiological protection characterised by a significant health improvement that may last for the duration of the transit: two and a half years. Health matters also concern various areas of life that need attention. Those represented by Saturn in the chart (House in Capricorn) and by Chiron (House in Virgo) are primarily concerned, while the benefit produced by Saturn may more particularly affect the areas represented by the House where Saturn transits.

Saturn in dissonance with Chiron
This transit seems to lower the ability of the body to respond to treatment in case of an illness. Saturn slows down and restricts the process of physiological and psychological recovery. The backdrop of this period is coloured with shades of grey, although other transits may bring light, life, and optimism in various ways. The areas

represented by both planets in the chart (Houses in Capricorn and Virgo) are primarily concerned. The discordance may be somehow linked to the areas represented by the House where Saturn transits.

Saturn in harmony with Uranus

This kind of transit has a beneficial and long-lasting influence on the ability to change, to innovate and to invent. The past, represented by Saturn, plays a positive role to favour the evolution to the future represented by Uranus. A rational approach to major ideas allows concrete realisation that may profoundly change life, more so in the areas represented by both planets in the chart (Houses in Capricorn and Aquarius) with positive motivation stemming from the areas represented by the House where Saturn transits.

Saturn in dissonance with Uranus

Changes are either stopped or imposed by unforeseen circumstances. The past plays a discordant role that does not seem to favour the future, or at least not as expected. Patience and determination are the best qualities to resist and eventually reach important goals despite the obstacles to overcome. The areas represented by both planets in the chart (Houses in Capricorn and Aquarius) are primarily concerned. Some of the reasons for such deceleration of pace can also affect the areas represented by the House where Saturn transits.

Saturn in harmony with Neptune

Dreams may come true during this period. Saturn enhances rationality and its constructive influence on imagination, inspiration, and dreams. The areas represented by both planets in the chart (Houses in Capricorn and Pisces) seem primarily concerned, as well as the House where Saturn transits. The endurance and determination shown to hang on to the dream greatly benefit the potential to obtain concrete results with long-lasting positive consequences. This is particularly strong when this period follows a dissonant transit that has created various challenges and setbacks for a couple of years prior to the present one.

Saturn in dissonance with Neptune

Dreams will come true, but it will take time to get concrete results. During this period, patience and determination are needed to overcome various obstacles and deal with a slowing down of pace with delays and other frustrating setbacks. The areas represented by both planets (Houses in Capricorn and Pisces) are primarily concerned as well as those represented by the House where Saturn transits. It is advised not to lose faith and to keep on going whatever happens. This is especially so if this dissonance is due to a transiting square because a transiting trine will follow with the positive influence mentioned in the previous aphorism.

Saturn in harmony with Pluto

This kind of transit is an excellent asset to strengthen the potential to regenerate, to sustain physical and psychological pressure, and to keep on going no matter what may come in the way of progress. The areas represented by both planets in the chart (Houses in Capricorn and Scorpio) are primarily concerned and favoured. They can positively affect the areas represented by the House where Saturn transits. Rebuilding or consolidating an existing situation enhances its robustness durably.

Saturn in dissonance with Pluto

Contrary to what is written above, this type of transit tends to slow down and reduce the ability to regenerate, both physically and psychologically. The grey colour of Saturn mixes with Pluto's black to create a dark period during which major transformations are likely to be fatefully resented. The areas represented by both planets in the chart (Houses in Capricorn and Scorpio) are primarily concerned, although some of the issues may come from the sectors of life represented by the House where Saturn transits.

Saturn in harmony with the Ascendant

This type of transit has a consolidating influence on the inner self, as it increases self-confidence in favour of a more rational and more constructive approach to life in the areas represented by Saturn in the chart (House in Capricorn). Some of the benefit comes from the areas represented by the House where Saturn transits. The role of this positive influence of Saturn is to help build up or reinforce important personal, social, or professional partnerships.

Saturn in dissonance with the Ascendant

Discouragement is often produced by this type of transit. The restricting influence of Saturn is felt within and without, both personally and in important relationships. Work gives unsatisfying results. Health may also be impaired due to a tendency to let go, rather than to stand up and fight. The areas represented by Saturn in the chart (House in Capricorn) and the areas represented by the House where Saturn transits are primarily concerned as the source of disappointment and disillusion. However, the time factor plays a major providential role that will be observed as soon as the dissonant aspect transforms into a harmonious one.

Saturn in harmony with the MidHeaven

The positive influence of Saturn is concretely useful to obtain better results at work and in any important project and situations. More determined and steady, the will becomes a source of solid motivation that allows reaching higher objectives. Climbing up the ladder is usually favoured by a beneficial transit of Jupiter, but Saturn produces longer-lasting results and satisfaction. Work and efforts are rewarded and positively affect the areas represented by Saturn in the chart (House in Capricorn) thanks to the constructive energy issued from the areas represented by the House where Saturn transits.

Saturn in dissonance with the MidHeaven

During this type of transit, climbing to the top and reaching goals takes longer and is more difficult. There may be some professional setbacks with their incidence at home and I personal relationships. Less motivation creates delays with their impact on the development and realisation of important projects. The areas represented by Saturn in the chart (House in Capricorn) are primarily concerned and sometimes responsible for the struggles that also affect the areas represented by the House where Saturn transits.

Lesson 4

CHIRON

Chiron is a name given to an asteroid or comet residue trapped between Saturn and Uranus by the powerful energy fields of these giant planets. Chiron was discovered in 1977. It takes about fifty one years to complete a full circle around the zodiac.

In mythology, Chiron is one of the centaurs, half-man, half-horse monsters, aggressive and devoid of intelligence ... Two of them, however, are beneficent. They are Chiron and Pholus. Chiron is the son of Cronos (Saturn). He is thoroughly familiar with the art of hunting, warfare, medicine and even music ...

Unfortunately, during a fight against evil entities the god Heracles unwillingly injures Chiron. Despite the care given, the wound does not heal. Chiron, an immortal entity, pushed to the limit by the dreadful pain, demands death. He obtains it from mortal Prometheus with whom he exchanges his immortality ...

Its accidental position between Saturn and Uranus makes Chiron the symbolic link between the two cosmic and mythological giants. From an astrological point of view, sedentarism, conservatism and sectarianism represented by Saturn become independence, freedom, and originality under the influence of Uranus. Chiron plays the role of intermediary between these tendencies uneasily coexisting in human nature. Chiron is the connection between the old and the young, the past and the future, traditions, and revolutions ...

Chiron is referred to as the "wounded healer". Its role is usually considered in relation to health. To me, it should be granted rulership of the sixth House in a chart and to the sixth sign, Virgo.

From my research and observations, it appears that Chiron represents the capacity to analyse, to observe, to focus on details, and to criticise and self-criticise. It is also important on a karmic point of view. Unlike Saturn which imposes blockages and obstacles necessary to progress and become stronger and efficient, Chiron compels deep reflection and self-evaluation. It represents the awareness derived from the ability to learn and to "heal" physiologically, and psychologically.

Chiron takes between fifty and fifty-one years to complete a full circle around the zodiac. However, the time spent transiting each sign is very different from one to another. This is due to its eccentric orbit around the Sun. For example, Chiron spends around eight years in Pisces, but only two years in Virgo.

THE CONJUNCTION

The transits of Chiron are not frequent, but they can last a long time. The return to its radical (original) position in the chart happens between 50 and 51 years of age. A second return concerns a minority of people who live to be over 100.

At 50 or 51, many people develop worrying pathologies. It is an important moment in life. Being over half a century old is a concern for some and a new beginning for others. The time has come to ponder and reflect on the reality of earthly existence. Major changes may be in store to make life more interesting or more preoccupying, depending on health concerns as much as on the level of intellectual and philosophical development.

The organs and functions represented by the sign where Chiron is in the birth chart are primarily concerned and may become a source of complications il they have not been correctly looked after since the early stages of life. Confronting such disorders may become an absolute necessity.

The return of Chiron is therefore linked to the need to improve wellbeing by taking important dietary or exercise decisions. To free the body from various sources of pollution is a positive source of motivation that can protect and greatly improve health both physically and psychologically.

Long before its return "home" described above, Chiron acts on itself in harmonious and discordant manners depending on the transiting aspects formed with its natal position in the chart. Contrary to Jupiter and Saturn, due to Chiron eccentric orbit, it is not possible to make a list of ages corresponding to any of the transiting aspects. To find out when Chiron was or will be in aspect with its position in a chart, the book of ephemeris is necessary. I recommend this one that you can buy online or at your local bookstore.

In this book, you will notice how different the durations of Chiron's transits are from one sign to another.

Take note of the periods of important passed transiting aspects and compare them with what happened, referring to the areas represented by Chiron in your chart.

You will also note the dates of important future transiting aspects to forecast the periods during which much may happen in relation with Chiron's original influence in your life.

THE HALF-SEXTILE

Check the ephemeris to find out when this type of aspect between Chiron and its original position in the chart occurs.

The first one can occur at a very young age, when the toddler is quite vulnerable to health issues and other problems.

The second one happens at around 46 years of age, before the return of Chiron on its original position. It is a period of doubt about many aspects of life, about health and about the areas represented by the House in Virgo and the House where Chiron is in the birth chart. It prepares for the return of Chiron explained in the paragraph about the conjunction.

THE SEXTILE

For a person born in 1950, with Chiron in Sagittarius, the first transiting sextile with its original position in the chart occurs at around 9 years of age, the second one at 42, the third one at 59 and the last one at 92.

For a person born in 1970, with Chiron in Aries, the first sextile occurs at around 16 years of age, the second one at 29, the third one at 65 and the fourth one at around 79. A fifth one could eventually occur at about 115 years of age ...

Similar differences apply to all other transiting aspects formed by Chiron with its original position in the chart. That is why it is not possible to establish a chart such as the ones proposed in the preceding chapters for Jupiter and Saturn.

The sextile has a beneficial influence on the general state of health as well as on the intellectual development, the ability to focus and understand more coherently.

The first sextile occurs during childhood or adolescence. The intellect becomes more rational and objective. Self-awareness is more obvious, innate potentials are more evident and what is learned is applied more logically than emotionally.

The other sextiles are every time linked to periods of evolution of consciousness of the self and of others around. The areas of life represented by the Houses transited by Chiron are primarily concerned. Improvement in such areas is linked to better self-control and organisation. The ability to heal is also enhanced physiologically and in other ways depending on the situation and the role of Chiron in the birth chart.

THE SQUARE

The transiting square in a dissonant aspect. When Chiron transits a sign belonging to an element that is not compatible with the element of its radical sign position, it produces a conflict of energies with detrimental consequences on the general state of health and in the areas represented by the Houses concerned.

The durations of such transits vary greatly between individuals due to Chiron's eccentric orbit, as explained earlier. The longer, the more difficult, although it seems to allow to get accustomed to the influence and manage it better.

The square warns about the potential unpleasant consequences of unhealthy habits. It is useful to understand and how to deal with difficulties rather than remain a victim of fatality. This notion applies also to the areas represented by the Houses concerned.[5]

The first square formed by Chiron with its own position in the chart marks a period during which rules and laws are a source of negative reactions. Uncomfortable about oneself makes it difficult to keep in tune with others who often are a truthful mirror. Conflicts are frequent due to a tendency to scrutinise, analyse, and criticise that cannot favour harmonious cohabitation. Abruptness and impetuosity colour a time when young age is a source of inner questioning and uncertainty.

The second square occurs at 45 or more. Profound changes of attitude have been imposed by difficulties with their influence on the evolution of personality. There is an unavoidable necessity to deal with life in a totally different manner. When it coincides with the transiting opposition of Uranus with itself in the chart, the second square of Chiron has a much greater impact. Radical changes occur. They are meant to open onto new horizons. They are the ultimate tests of this middle-age period after which nothing will ever be the same again.

The third square happens at around 60 or more. Retirement is in the air, but it is not always a joyous perspective. It is harvest time. If it coincides with the second return of Saturn explained in the

---

[5] The Houses concerned are the House where Chiron transits, the House where it is found in the chart, and the House in Virgo.

previous chapter, health may become an issue or an important subject that motivates major decisions to preserve or restore wellbeing. Reorganisation of life is often linked to a change of social or professional status. Sixty is not old but it is a fact that most of one's life is behind, not forward in terms of time left to live. It therefore becomes necessary to build a new future to be enjoyed as long as possible. Knowing that a trine follows this square makes this period more bearable and promising in terms of the good and pleasant surprises that life keeps in store for us in various ways.

The fourth square occurs in the early eighties. Health is often a greater source of concern. The average human lifespan is reached. There are many exceptions of course. The fourth square corresponds to the last warning on the necessity to take care of the existential vehicle to take it farther along the road of life. Because it happens that simultaneously Uranus returns to its original position, it gives Chiron a more important effect on physiological functions and on the general state of mind. Other important transits occur during this period. Jupiter, for example, returns to its original position for the seventh time, and Saturn forms a square with its original position at around 80 years of age, while Neptune forms an opposition to its natal position. Those are some of the reasons that make the early eighties a critical period during which extra care and caution are necessary to preserve health and wellbeing.

To know for sure when Chiron forms various aspects with its own position in a chart, use the ephemeris. Do not rely on the approximate figures given in this lesson.

THE TRINE

The periods during which Chiron forms a trine with its own position in the birth chart are known as being quite favourable in various ways. Its positive energy is particularly remarkable in the areas represented by the House in Virgo and the House transited by Chiron. There seems to be more resistance to illness and more efficiency to deal with challenges occurring in these areas of life.

The first transiting trine formed by Chiron with its original position occurs at different times in life from one person to another because of the eccentric orbit of this object. It can be expected between 18 and 26 years of age when enthusiasm is derived from the many projects and ambitions a young person has at that age. Studying may be the best way to make good use of the observation and focussing abilities derived from Chiron. Many other benefits are derived from this important transit too often overlooked by astrologers.

The second transiting trine occurs at around 40 years of age[6]. Mature but still young and alert, the person is involved in important projects and can envision the future based on past experiences and ambitions. Chiron allows a more rational approach and vision of reality. It helps understand more complex problems to find adequate solutions. Difficulties do not disappear by magic, but they are more easily and efficiently addressed. Realism and self-criticism allow better adaptability to important circumstances.

The areas of life represented by Chiron in the birth chart (House in Virgo) and by the House where it is transiting, are primarily concerned. See also what you can derive from the areas represented by the House position of the ruler of the sign transited by Chiron[7] to enlarge the field of investigation and enrich the analysis of the transit.

The third transiting trine occurs at about 70 years of age. Its influence is useful to protect health and preserve from the always possible ailments stemming from an aging body and mind. Chiron helps decide what to do to improve physical and psychological strength. Its beneficial influence is particularly appreciated to recover from illness as well as to solution important problems in the areas represented by Chiron in the birth chart (House in Virgo) and by the House where it is transiting. Many people enjoy life greatly

---

[6] Check the ephemeris to know for sure.

[7] A transiting planet in a sign is subject to the influence of the ruler of that sign. Its position in the chart is an important element to enrich the interpretation of the transit.

in their seventies. The better they look after their health and their state of affairs, the longer they can enjoy their freedom … Of course, Chiron is not a magic wand than can make miracles. It is just a positive influence that can increase the ability to analyse and understand what needs to be done to improve the quality of life objectively and wisely.

THE INCONJUNCT

The energy of the inconjunct is comparable to Chiron's influence because it represents an inner dilemma with its troubling influence on the ability to decide. Chiron represents the potential to see things as they are, but it does not confer the ability to act accordingly until it becomes absolutely necessary to do so.

The age reached when an inconjunct is formed between transiting Chiron and its position in the birth chart are very different from one person to another because of its eccentric orbit. That is why it is essential to use the ephemeris mentioned earlier to determine when the inconjunct occurs.

Example: for someone born with Chiron in Sagittarius, the first transiting inconjunct with its original position occurs when Chiron is in Taurus, at around 30 years of age. The second transiting inconjunct occurs ten years later, in the early forties.

By comparison, for someone born with Chiron in Cancer, the first transiting inconjunct occurs at about 10, when Chiron is in Sagittarius, and the second one only six years later, at 16 years of age …

When transiting Chiron produces an inconjunct with its original position in the chart, health may become a source of concerns, but there may be no remarkable warnings to alert and motivate a medical consultation. A tendency to avoid direct confrontation tempers the ability and desire to react immediately. On the contrary, Chiron can also create an inclination to exaggerate and to feel overly threatened by the faintest symptom …

The period of transiting inconjuncts are marked by ambiguity in other forms and areas, depending on the House ruled by Chiron in the birth chart and the House where it is transiting.

The need to analyse and focus on petty details is emphasised by fear and insecurity. Mistakes are made due to lack of realism that enhances a feeling of inadequacy in the areas mentioned above.

The first and second inconjuncts have different astrological meanings. The first one precedes a transiting opposition, while the second one is followed by a trine. It is important to take note of the type of inconjunct concerned to improve your analysis of this transit.

THE OPPOSITION

Although Chiron takes between fifty and fifty-one years to come back to its original position in the chart, it does not mean that it forms an opposition with itself at around 25 years of age. Once again, this is due to its eccentric orbit around the Sun.

For example, Chiron in Sagittarius at birth forms an opposition with itself when it transits in Gemini at 36 years of age. The second opposition occurs at around 86.

By comparison, Chiron in Cancer forms an opposition with its own position at around 13 years of age, an a second one at around 63.

The opposition is like a mirror in which the meaning of Chiron is reflected. It is a reversed image that underlines the flaws and imperfections represented by its position in the chart. Chiron has a karmic meaning. It represents lessons to learn while solving existential dilemmas. A greater need to take notice of the importance of being in good health, really or symbolically, emerges during the transiting opposition.

The opposition should be interpreted as a warning. During this period, unsettling realities are exposed. Chiron shows the flip side of the medal to highlight our hidden qualities and flaws. When it occurs at about thirteen years of age, it perdures during most of the teenage years enhancing the inner turmoil of the young person. Being confronted to oneself tends to marginalise, making the transition to adulthood more difficult.

Chiron's logic is implacable because of its karmic nature unfathomable for a young soul. Teenage suffering impacts a whole generation of people who mature too early and confront bitterly their elders' way of life.

When transiting Chiron forms an opposition with a planet or other element in the chart, it corresponds to a period when we are confronted to important responsibilities represented by the element concerned. Chiron invites and incites us to see things as they are rather than how we have been accustomed to look at them.

It becomes necessary to be in phase with the areas of life concerned. The opposition is an axis around which we need to turn to understand its deeper meaning and value. Choices have to be made. They are designed to avoid regrettable mistakes and their long-term consequences often remarked when Chiron returns to its original position, twenty-five years later …

12/01/1967 18:00

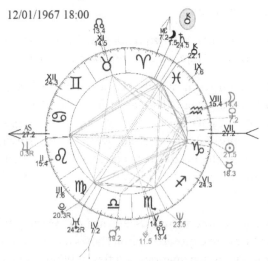

In this chart, the transit of Chiron at the end of Pisces and early Aries plays a major role in this person's life. The opposition with the conjunction Uranus-Pluto shows how necessary it becomes to accept great changes to benefit from the sextiles and trines in the birth chart reactivated during this transit.

Chiron and the other elements in the chart

During its revolution around the zodiac, Chiron connects successively with all the elements present in your birth chart. I have included a list of aphorisms to help you analyse the possible influence of transiting Chiron. They are classified in two sections: harmonious and *dissonant* aspects. Use them only as guides. If you simply copy-paste these short interpretations, you are likely to be far off the true meaning of Chiron's transits.

THE TRANSITING ASPECTS OF CHIRON

Chiron in harmony with the Sun

This type of transit is a source of positive energy that protects health, both physically and psychologically. It confers a more rational approach to life and an improved ability to focus on details and avoid errors due to lack of attention. Chiron is also useful to deal with authority and various responsibilities more efficiently in the areas represented by the House in Leo and Virgo.

Chiron in dissonance with the Sun

It is advised to exercise extra caution to avoid various disorders and other setbacks during this period. This may be more remarkable in the areas represented by the Houses in Leo and Virgo, and by the House where Chiron transits. Negligence is a source of errors that interfere with the realisation of important projects. Health concerns often become the centre of attention during this type of transit.

Chiron in harmony with the Moon

This transit improves the ability to control emotions and to divert greater benefit from the association of personal feelings and rational thinking. It also protects health and favours recovery from eventual illness. The areas represented by the Houses in Cancer and Virgo, and by the House where Chiron transits benefit from more efficient and emotional self-control that promotes success and wellbeing.

Chiron in dissonance with the Moon

This type of transit affects the glandular system, the digestion, and the control of emotions. A tendency to worry too much increases disorders and their distressing influence both physically and psychologically. The areas represented by the Houses in Cancer and Virgo, and by the House where Chiron transits are subject to emotional surges of uncertainty and errors of judgement.

Chiron in harmony with Mercury

This transit is particularly beneficial to the cognitive functions. It improves the intellect and confers an accrued ability to focus and to analyse. It is useful while studying, travelling and in all situations where communication and mental accuracy are most important assets. The areas represented by the Houses in Gemini and Virgo, and the House transited by Chiron benefit from the positive influence of this transit on the intellect and rational thinking.

Chiron in dissonance with Mercury

This kind of transit indicates intellectual disorders that may affect objectivity in the areas represented by the Houses in Gemini and Virgo, and the House where Chiron transits. A special effort is necessary to avoid losing track, forgetting, and getting mentally confused in presence of adversity. Mental work loses efficiency, while communication is a source of misunderstandings.

Chiron in harmony with Venus

This transit confers an accrued ability to deal with love and feelings in a rational way to enjoy the good things of life in the areas represented by the Houses in Taurus and Virgo, and the House where Chiron transits. Creativity is better controlled and becomes a source of concrete realisations in various ways. Chiron protects various functions such as the thyroid or the reproductive organs.

Chiron in dissonance with Venus

Health concerns may centre around the reproductive and thyroid functions. This transit tends to increase a tendency to worry too much and to feel sentimentally more vulnerable or inadequate. Focusing on petty details may also create loss of self-confidence in the areas represented by both planets in the chart (Houses in Taurus and Virgo) and the House where Chiron transits.

Chiron in harmony with Mars

This period is marked by an improved efficiency to act and react. Better use of the analysing potential is an asset to obtain great results in the areas represented by both planets in the chart (Houses in Aries and Virgo) and by the House where Chiron transits. The influence of Chiron is also useful to deal with and treat possible health concerns. The appreciation of smaller details improves efficiency at work and in various other situations.

Chiron in dissonance with Mars

During this type of transit, it is necessary to think before acting or deciding on important matters and situations. A tendency to worry may produce mistakes due to bad timing or unexpected turns of events. Muscle, joints, or digestive pains are also possible. The areas represented by both planets (Houses in Aries and Virgo) and by the House where Chiron transits are primarily concerned.

Chiron in harmony with Vesta

This transit seems to have a beneficial influence on health condition, whether there is a concern or not. It confers a better understanding of the necessity to look after oneself to preserve a positive physical and psychological equilibrium. The ability to analyse and understand is also a valuable asset in the areas represented by the Houses in Virgo and Libra, and by the House where Chiron transits.

Chiron in dissonance with Vesta

Loss of balance, both physiologically and psychologically is sometimes observed during this type of transit. There is a tendency to worry about health that affects latent potentials with detrimental consequences in the areas represented by the Houses in Virgo and Libra, and by the House where Chiron is transiting. Mental and physical harmonisation techniques may become necessary.

Chiron in harmony with Jupiter

This type of transit allows more judicious use of opportunities thanks to the analysing capacity and the order in which decisions are taken to derive various satisfactions from the better things in life. Health may also benefit from this transit. The areas represented by both planets (Houses in Virgo and Sagittarius) and the House where Chiron is transiting are primarily concerned and favoured.

Chiron in dissonance with Jupiter

This transit enhances an innate inclination to focus on distressing details that may increase the importance of various issues rather than help find satisfying solutions. Health may become a source of worry due to a tendency to exaggerate or ignore alerting symptoms. The areas represented by both planets in the chart (Houses in Virgo and Sagittarius) and the House where Chiron is transiting are primarily implicated. Relaxation or meditation is advised.

Chiron in harmony with Saturn

This type of transit is a source of accrued ability to make the necessary effort to reach goals and realise important projects. It renders more efficient, patient, and resilient to surmount obstacles and obtain positive results with long-lasting consequences. The areas represented by the Houses in Virgo and Capricorn, and the House where Chiron transits are primarily concerned.

Chiron in dissonance with Saturn

This transit may affect the ability to resist and make concrete decisions to deal with various issues that may have their roots in a long-distant past. Health may be affected by fatigue and lack of physical and psychological activity. The areas represented by both planets in the chart (Houses in Virgo and Capricorn) and the Houses where Chiron is transiting are primarily affected.

Chiron in harmony with Chiron

This transit allows better understanding of the importance of physical and psychological wellbeing. Health is taken more seriously and is efficiently looked after to improve life in various ways. The areas represented by the House in Virgo and the House where Chiron transits benefit from the enhanced ability to take advantage of fortunate opportunities concretely and durably.

Chiron in dissonance with Chiron

This type of transit indicates a period during which a tendency to worry too much or too little about health may increase the risk of illness. The overall approach to physical and psychological wellbeing may be responsible for distress and confusion. The areas represented by the House in Virgo and by the House where Chiron transits are primarily concerned and in need of attention.

Chiron in harmony with Uranus

This transit corresponds to a period during which what needs to be changed, renewed, transformed, or updated benefit from accrued mental efficiency and analysing capacity. Well planned, changes become a source of durable satisfaction and positive motivation. The areas represented by the Houses in Virgo and Aquarius, and the House where Chiron is transiting are primarily concerned.

Chiron in dissonance with Uranus

During this transits, errors of judgement may produce unexpected and undesirable changes. The need of a more realistic approach to life is challenged by lack of efficiency and motivation. Health can become a source of sudden concerns. Unforeseen issues are likely to disrupt the areas represented by the Houses in Virgo and Capricorn, and the House where Chiron is transiting in the chart.

Chiron in harmony with Neptune

This transit is favourable to the realisation of dreams or far-fetched projects. The positive relationship between imagination, sensibility and rationalism allows more efficiency to obtain better results in the areas represented by the Houses in Virgo and Pisces, and the House where Chiron is transiting. The natural connection with the spiritual dimension of life may also become a source of creative inspiration.

Chiron in dissonance with Neptune

Dreams seem more difficult to realise due to a tendency to analyse and worry too much about the outcomes of various projects and situations. Irrational anxiety about health is likely. Treatments may not give the expected results. The areas represented by the Houses in Virgo and Pisces, and by the House where Chiron transits are primarily concerned and in need of more rationalism than emotivity.

Chiron in harmony with Pluto

The ability to regenerate is accentuated during this type of transit. Chiron confers more efficiency to deal with what needs to be profoundly reviewed and transformed. Health benefits from a more positive and rational approach to occasional issues. The areas represented by the Houses in Virgo and Scorpio, and by the House where Chiron transits are well supported during this period.

Chiron in dissonance with Pluto

This type of transit tends to affect the regenerating capacity of the body to fight occasional issues. It represents a period of morosity and existential concern. Health may be affected, while the areas represented by the Houses in Virgo and Scorpio, and by the House where Chiron is transiting need deep restructuration.

Chiron in harmony with the Ascendant

During this transit, understanding and analysing the deeper need of the self are a source of progress and positive results. Healthier habits may contribute to improvement or restoration of wellbeing. The areas represented by the House in Virgo and the House where Chiron is transiting have a strong influence that motivates and favours personal achievements in various ways.

Chiron in dissonance with the Ascendant

Health may become a source of concern with its detrimental influence on the expression of the self. Uncertainty and lack of optimism result in loss of motivation and a tendency to be too rational or too pessimistic. The areas represented by the House is Virgo and the House where Chiron transits play a dominant role. It is advised to cultivate a more positive approach to personal needs.

Chiron in harmony with the Mid-Heaven

Social or professional achievements are favoured by a more efficient use of the intellect and ability to rational thinking. Better organisation produces better results. Ambitious projects are a source of motivation and potentially greater success. The areas represented by the House in Virgo and the House where Chiron transits play a major role in the social or professional progress during this period.

Chiron in dissonance with the Mid-Heaven

Intellectual efficiency is a must to obtain the best results at work and in personal projects and realisations. During this kind of transit, it seems more difficult to analyse rationally and organise what needs to be done to deal with important tasks. The areas represented by the House in Virgo and the House where Chiron transits may play a major role in developing pessimism to the detriment of success.

Once again, remember that these short aphorisms are only a guide. They need to be blended with the other transits that may enhance or limit the influence of Chiron as it progresses around a birth chart.

A transit affects different elements differently. For example, transiting Chiron may be in dissonance with the Sun and in harmony with Jupiter. The meanings of both transits tend to contradict one-another, not mentioning the other transiting influences occurring simultaneously around the chart …

The task is to blend and synthesize all influences to obtain a proper prognosis.

Lesson 5

URANUS

Uranus is the seventh planet of the solar system by its distance to the Sun. It is the third one by its size and the fourth one by its mass. Its name is taken from the Greek deity, Ouranos, father of Saturn and grand-father of Jupiter. He is the god of the skies, also father of Mercury and Venus. Uranus hated his children, and immediately after their birth, he confined them in Tartarus, in consequence of which he was unmanned and dethroned by Cronos at the instigation of Gaea[8] …

Below is the list of transiting aspects produced by Uranus with its own position in the chart at various ages during a lifetime.

Conjunction	Sextiles	Squares	Trines	Opposition	Inconjuncts
age	age	age	age	age	age
84	14 and 70	21 and 63	31 and 53	42	35 and 49

Uranus represents the electrochemical energy needed for neuronal and other cellular functions. Without it, the cortex and grey matter would be useless and lifeless. Uranus acts on the nervous system with lightning-fast repercussions on physical and psychological levels. Drastic changes occurring during a transit of Uranus are definitive and irreversible.

Uranus is much slower than Saturn, Chiron, and Jupiter. It completes one full circle around the zodiac in eighty-four years. Only one conjunction with its original position is therefore possible during a

---

[8] For more information, visit this site:
https://www.theoi.com/Protogenos/Ouranos.html

human life cycle. This is an important moment when changes may deeply affect health and the life force. Its influence becomes progressively more intense from around 80 years of age and it continues to produce unexpected physical and psychological effects until 87 to 90 years of age.

From the moment of birth, the transits of Uranus produce various radical modifications in the areas represented by the House in Aquarius and the Houses represented by the other planets concerned during such transits. Uranus transits through one complete sign in seven years.

The transits of Uranus play a dominant role when major aspects are produced with its own position in the chart. Their meanings and their effects must be taken into consideration to establish a proper forecast.

THE CONJUNCTION

As indicated earlier in this lesson, only one conjunction is possible between Uranus and its own position in the chart. It occurs at 84 years of age, but its influence begins earlier and lasts until the conjunction is too large to be considered as such. Although most astrologers do not, I consider that the influence of the conjunction perdures for the duration of the transit of Uranus in the sign concerned.

Uranus transits through a complete sign in seven years. However, the time when the influence of the conjunction begin depends on the original position of Uranus in the birth chart. It usually starts to be strong as soon as it enters in the sign, even if its own position in the chart is at the end of that sign. In this case, the influence of the conjunction can be felt up to seven years before the true aspect at 84 years of age.

Example: *If in a birth chart Uranus is at 1° in a sign, it will be submitted to the influence of its return as soon as it enters into that sign, at 84 years of age.*

If Uranus is at 29° in a sign, the influence of its return is felt almost seven years before, at 77 years of age, although the exact conjunction always occurs at 84.

This is based on the fact that the energy of a planet in transit spreads through the entire sign as soon as it enters it, affecting all planets, objects, and elements present in that sign.

The return of Uranus is a unique event that produces radical changes in relation to its original position and the aspects with other elements in the chart. Although health may be primarily affected, it is not an absolute rule. Uranus also strongly affects the areas of life represented by the House in Aquarius and the House where it transits because it is also the House where it was at birth.

The return of Uranus brings "something" back from a long distant past in relation with important events dating back from the first year of life.

To me, the birth chart is the first "solar return" chart. As such, it represents what the newborn has been exposed to while still in a vegetative state of human development. It is a crucial period during which what happens is not memorised and analysed mentally. Memories are stored in the cells where they create chain reactions that influence the psychological and physical development.

To illustrate the influence of the return of Uranus, see the example chart on the next page. This person, born on 15 June 1943, passed away on 5 December 2017. In a chart, the Ascendant represents the moment of birth. Its position is determined by the combination of the date, place, and especially the time of birth.

The zodiac circle is made up of 360° (degrees), while a year is made up of 365 days. It can therefore be said that one degree around the zodiac circle equals one day. To be precise: $1° = 1.014$ days.

From the position of the Ascendant, every portion of thirty degrees is approximately equivalent to one month (thirty days). I have written the different dates all around the chart. Each one begins near the first degree of a sign.

Planets and other objects or elements have their own energy that interact via the aspects. The configurations produced represent various events, situations, or incidents, depending on the type of aspect (harmonious or dissonant).

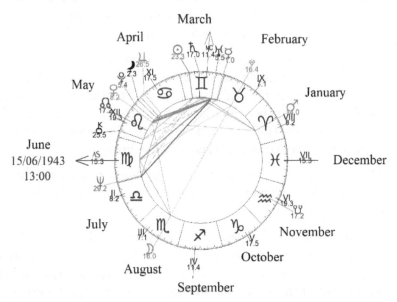

About Uranus (♅), you can see it in Gemini, conjunct Mercury and forming various aspects with other elements in the chart. There is a large square with the Ascendant, a trine with Neptune and sextiles with Lilith, Venus, and Pluto in Leo.

The conjunction Mercury/Uranus corresponds to the early days of March 1944, eight and a half months after birth.

Mercury is the ruler of Gemini, the solar sign of this person. The Sun is therefore in Gemini. Both the Mid Heaven (House X) and the Sun represent the father and, by extension, the relationship with authority, hierarchy, and masculinity. Uranus rules House VI (Health and work) in Aquarius. Its presence in Gemini indicates pulmonary vulnerability. The lungs are represented by Gemini in medical astrology.

This male child was abandoned, first by his father, then by his mother. The father was an unpredictable, original man who led a bohemian, marginal life. He left his wife and a child only eight-month old. To make his action even worse morally, he stole his baby's cot and some of his clothes to try and sell them because he needed a bit of money to carry on his mediocre project...

We can imagine that such an important event drastically and suddenly changed the newborn's life in that morning of March 1944. Health may have also been a concern. It was wartime in Paris and his mum did not have much money to take care of her baby alone. That is why she left the toddler to her sister and went to work as a model, promising to soon come back. She never did...

Seventy-two years later, in 2016, lung cancer was diagnosed. It probably had begun long before the symptoms became too much for this impetuous individual to handle.

It is important from an astrological point of view because Uranus transited the position of Mars at 14° in Aries, ruler of House VIII in House VIII in February 2015. Uranus, ruler of House VI (work and health) was transiting the ruler of House VIII (death) for the first and last time in this person's life. Knowing that Uranus is conjunct Mercury in Gemini in the birth chart, it shows how much the pulmonary function was concerned by the disturbing influence of transiting Uranus. The link between health and death is established with such force for the first time since the events of March 1944 ...

By transiting the position of Mars, Uranus brought back the stress felt seventy-one years earlier. If this person had survived the illness, the next troubling period would have been produced by the arrival of Uranus at the longitude of Vesta (ruler of House IV, the mother and family background) bringing back other emotionally stressful memories to the man's body and soul where they were stored for so many years...

This example illustrates the powerful influence of Uranus in transit.

THE HALF SEXTILE

As explained earlier, I consider the half-sextile differently than most of my fellow astrologers. A half-sextile precedes the conjunction, and a second one follows that same conjunction. The first one is a period of preparation to the effect of the conjunction. The second one is a period of liberation from the conjunction. Therefore, the dissonances between the elements of the signs involved act differently in both cases.

Example: In a birth chart, Uranus transits in Taurus and forms a half-sextile with the Sun in Gemini. It takes seven years for Uranus to go from the half-sextile to the conjunction. This is the period given to prepare for the conjunction, a very important transiting aspect. There may be some apprehension and worry because of the great changes Uranus is likely to produce when it reaches the position of the Sun in the chart. During those seven years, other transits occur. They must be taken into consideration year after year to determine more precisely how the energy of Uranus can be put to good use rather than fall victim of it ...

The half-sextile that follows the transit of Uranus in the solar sign corresponds to a period of deliverance following major changes produced by the influence of Uranus during the seven years prior to this half-sextile. It is advised to exercise caution and prudence to avoid errors due to an exaggerated feeling of freedom. Seven years later, this second half-sextile becomes a sextile, allowing yet more freedom and perhaps a more efficient ability to benefit from what it has to deliver.

Note that this example concerns only the influence of Uranus in transiting conjunction with the position of the Sun in a birth chart. Remember that it simultaneously creates other aspects with other planets and elements around the chart. However, the Sun is the centre of the system. All objects in that system depend on it to be where and what they are. Therefore, what acts on the energy of the Sun influences the whole system. That is why the videos that I publish on the Internet each year for each sign of the zodiac are so appreciated. But of course, it does not mean that you should only concentrate on the transiting aspects formed with the Sun in a birth chart to deliver a proper forecast.

This law of alternance between + and - must be applied to all the transits of the other planets and objects or elements in movement around a birth chart. The Moon also creates a similar phenomenon during its two-and-a-half-day transit through a sign. That is why the Moon acts on our emotions, moods, physiological balance, lymphatic, and digestive functions.

THE SEXTILE and THE TRINE

When Uranus in transit produces a sextile and a trine with its own position in the chart, a long period of unexpected opportunities marked by beneficial changes often unplanned, but always welcomed. Reactivity and adaptability, inventiveness, and playability are enhanced with positive repercussions in the areas represented by the House in Aquarius and the House where Uranus is transiting.

The duration of the aspect varies. Like any other, it depends on the occasional retrogradations that can retain Uranus in the same area of the zodiac for many months. In retrograde motion, its influence is not as strong. It may even go into "standby" mode until it returns in direct movement.

To me, the effect of a transiting aspect lasts as long as the transit in the sign. For example, if Uranus is in Taurus at birth, it will benefit from the sextile for seven years, while it transits in Pisces or in Cancer.

I know that many astrologers do not agree with this theory, but I have verified it sufficiently often to apply it daily in all my readings successfully.

Although the sextile's reputations is to be half as beneficial as the trine, I rather think that it plays a different role. As explained in the lesson on Jupiter, the sextile links signs of spontaneously compatible elements: Fire and Air, Water and Earth, and vice-versa.

Therefore, when transiting Uranus forms a sextile with its own position in the chart, the beneficial influence can approximately last for seven years.

Why "approximately"?

Firstly, because of retrogradation periods and because of its original position in a sign, a transiting aspect (sextile or other) begins and ends differently.

An example:

For someone born with Uranus at 4° in Cancer, the sextile begins at 12 years of age, in Virgo. It will last only six years, when Uranus enters in Libra.

Use the chart proposed at the beginning of this chapter as a guide to memorise the approximate ages when Uranus creates such or such aspect with its own position. Verify in the ephemeris to confirm or to get a more precise and official information.

The transiting sextile period is usually marked by various happy events and beneficial changes. Although there may be setbacks and issues due to counteracting planetary transits from other planets, Uranus enhances adaptability and positive reactivity to deal with eventual problems and find original and often unexpected solutions.

The second sextile occurs much later, around the age of seventy. Positive changes usually occur after retirement. They are issued from the freedom that it allows. At 70 and more, the quality of life depends on what has been done (or not) to make this period a source of concrete satisfaction. It may be that Uranus brings back the consequence of the previous sextile dating back sixty years in terms of personal realisation prevented by professional, social, or family strife. Retirement is often compared to a new birth and a new life.

When the sextile becomes a half-sextile

As explained earlier, the half-sextile links two following signs. They belong to incompatible elements, just like the square and the inconjunct. That is why I consider the half-sextile as a dissonant aspect. Knowing that when it precedes a conjunction, it should be seen as a period of preparation to the return of the planet concerned to its original position. In the case of Uranus, it only happens once in a lifetime. When it precedes a sextile, it should also be viewed as a period of preparation to the beneficial changes the sextile promises.

During a transiting sextile that will eventually become a half-sextile, the period should be used to prepare for the disturbing effect of the half-sextile.

The half-sextile that follows the conjunction is a period marked by the drastic changes produced by the return of Uranus when old age makes life more uncertain and occasionally difficult in various ways. This transiting aspect lasts for seven years before it becomes a positive sextile toward the age of 94 …

The square follows the sextile and eventually becomes a trine. A planet is always connected to its original position in the chart. As it revolves around it, the type of transiting aspect produced shows how the energy of the planet expresses itself in accordance with the notions of harmony and dissonance.

THE SQUARE

The transiting square produced by Uranus with its own position or with other elements in the chart, usually imposes important changes in the areas represented by the House in Aquarius, by the House where Uranus transits, and the House/s ruled by the other planet/s involved.

Sudden unexpected and undesirable setbacks occur during a transiting square. The moments when Uranus form an exact aspect are marked by more important events. In case of a retrogradation, up to three occurrences are to be anticipated.

Meanwhile, more aspects are formed by transiting Uranus with the other elements of the chart. I have included a list of aphorisms at the end of this lesson to help you analyse such configurations.

As explained earlier, when you analyse a transiting aspect, always take note of the quality of the following one. Knowing that a square with its own position eventually turns into a trine, a trine into an inconjunct, an inconjunct into an opposition, and so on, allows to forecast beyond the limit of the forecast you are making.

Uranus takes seven years to transit a sign. It is a long time to wait for a square to become a sextile or a trine. By explaining what the sextile or trine positively produces, the period of the transiting square becomes easier to bear.

In the same manner, knowing that a trine becomes a square or an inconjunct alerts on the necessity to rip as much goodness off from the period of the transiting trine to make it easier to deal with the following square or inconjunct. It is like saving money while finances are good in prevision of less fortunate times. Remember, "what goes up must come down …"

In the example illustration on the following page, you can see that when Uranus transits in Gemini, moving from the square with its own position while it transits in Taurus, the square transforms into a sextile. The disrupting events linked to the square become a source of positive change when the sextile forms. Hence, the dissonant aspect loses some of its unpleasant influence by opening onto a more enjoyable forecast. The areas of life represented by the House where Uranus transits is affected in relation with the House in Aquarius.

In this chart, Uranus rules House IV in Aquarius and transits House VII in Taurus. It represents a period marked by destabilising events and unpleasant changes in family life and home environment with their disrupting consequences in marriage or other important relationship. Due to the original position in Leo in House IX near the Mid-Heaven, the career and social status are likely to be impacted by the situation at home.

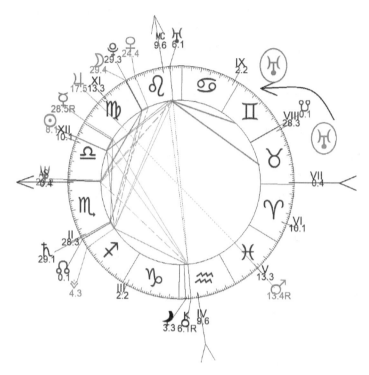

When it becomes a sextile, the influence or Uranus is much more enjoyable, but the degree of success and satisfaction derived from this aspect depends on how the influence of the square was dealt with when Uranus was is Taurus.

Due to the long time spent in a sign, Uranus imposes many changes during its seven-year transits. It is therefore crucial to mention in your readings that whatever an aspect is, it is always followed by a different one seven years later. *The same rule applies to all other planets in transits around the chart, especially the slower ones, from Jupiter to Pluto.*

THE INCONJUNCT

Two long periods of transiting inconjuncts occur in a lifetime. The first one between 31 and 38 years of age, and the second one between 46 and 53. As for all other transits, its influence is stronger when

Uranus is close to the exact aspect. You need to check the ephemeris to determine the period of inconjunct. Allow about 5° on each side of the exact aspect to ascertain the length of the transiting inconjunct.

Although the ambiguous effect of an inconjunct can perdure for up to seven years, its influence is naturally at its strongest when the angle formed by transiting Uranus with its original position is between 148° and 152°.

During this period, the desire to change is great, but it usually lacks concrete purpose and direction. There is hope and high expectations, but inconsistent efforts made to attain satisfactory results.

If the inconjunct precedes an opposition, existential abnormalities are perceived, but not spontaneously addressed. It confers that very human tendency to postpone until tomorrow what should be done immediately. That is why problems are likely to pile up and the overall situation is likely to become worse. When the succeeding long period of opposition occurs, its powerful energy can produce radical changes that profoundly destabilise and threaten the person's health and the areas represented by Uranus in the birth chart (House in Aquarius) and by the Houses where Uranus transits and where Uranus is positioned in the chart.

The transiting inconjunct that follows the opposition has a different meaning. Because it comes after a long period of opposition that has created radical changes, there may be a tendency to feel demotivated and tired, both physically and psychologically. Adapting to a new environment or a totally new situation is not easy. It takes time and courage to rebuild, renew, or renovate. Lack of motivation can lengthily delay concrete realisations and instil a feeling of inadequacy with its depressing consequences. Knowing that a transiting trine will follow is an encouraging positive point to raise when analysing the effect of this inconjunct.

The inconjunct is a karmic aspect. It has an enlightening connotation. When it precedes the opposition, it warns about major changes likely to occur and offers ample time (seven years) to prepare for such changes before they occur. When it precedes a trine, it shows what needs to be done while it lats so that the transiting trine's influence is as positive as possible.

Knowing that the inconjunct precedes a trine is more positive than to analyse it as following the opposition. The role of Uranus is linked to the future, not the past. What has been remains forever as such. Only the future can be changed ...

THE OPPOSITION

The "midlife crisis" occurs between the age of 40 and 45. In astrology it is symbolised by the transiting opposition of Uranus with its own position at 42 years of age.

It is a critical period when drastic changes often occur with irreversible consequences. The opposition is not to be considered as discordant as most astrologers believe it to be. When Uranus is opposed to its own position, major changes allow a complete transformation of life at various levels, mainly in the areas represented by the House in Aquarius, the House where Uranus is in the birth chart, and the opposite House where it transits.

The energy of the aspect culminates when the opposition reaches 180°, but its underlying influence lasts for the duration of the transit in the sign (seven years).

As explained for transiting Chiron versus its own position, the opposition is like a mirror that reflects a reversed image in which both qualities and flaws become more obvious and visible. Uranus opposing itself liberates the energy of change and exposes the true meaning of life by assembling both our visible and hidden sides.

If Uranus is positioned near the end of a sign in the birth chart, the energy of the opposition begins as soon as the planet enters that sign. From then on, its influence gradually increases until it reaches the true aspect (180°) seven years or so later. Knowing that the true aspect occurs at 42, it means that the effect of the opposition can begin up to seven years earlier, at 35 years of age. It also means that an important event occurring at 35 can wait until seven years later to produce drastic outcomes (at 42) …

On the contrary, if Uranus is positioned at the beginning of a sign in the birth chart, the influence of the opposition begins almost immediately, at 42 when a major event or drastic change can occur. Its effect can then linger on until the end of the transit of Uranus in the opposite sign, seven years later, at around 49 years of age.

It is therefore important to take note of the position of Uranus in the birth chart to establish a more valuable prognosis on its possible influence in the areas concerned. Remember that the transiting opposition of Uranus with its own position is a unique event that follows and precedes an inconjunct. I believe that the events occurring during the transiting opposition are often linked to what has not been dealt with properly during the preceding transiting inconjunct. The following transiting inconjunct represents a long period of uncertainty due to the revolutionary changes produced by the transiting opposition. What comes up must come down …

Does it mean that from the beginning of the first inconjunct until the end of the second one we can expect twenty-one difficult years? The karmic nature of the inconjunct could let us believe so. However, more that systematic difficulties, the three periods (inconjunct, opposition, inconjunct) are necessary to progress in many ways. The experience stemming from the various situations and events force us to surpass ourselves. What is rationally done gives rational results. What is left to fate to decide usually brings disillusion and regrets.

When Uranus is strong, its influence is greater, but it is perhaps also easier to deal with, especially if it is the dominant planet of the birth chart. In any case, always remember to link the transits of the planets you analyse to the Houses they represent, the House where they are positioned in the birth chart, and the Houses where they transit.

Uranus and the other elements in the chart

Radical changes are to be expected in the areas represented by the planet in aspect with transiting Uranus. The quality of such changes depends on the type of aspect produced during the transit. Such changes may be stored and inactive until a faster planet forms a conjunction with the slower planet in transit. That faster transit serves as a trigger to the event produced by the transit of the slow planet.

All transiting aspects of Uranus with the rest of the chart occur only once in a lifetime, or at least from birth until 84 years of age. The eventual second occurrences after 84 are lived much differently. Note that when we turn 84, while Uranus comes back to its original position, Saturn is about to do the same for the third time (at 87) while Neptune and Pluto are transiting opposite their initial positions.

It therefore makes sense to consider this period as quite challenging. Adding to the various existential difficulties in the areas represented by the Houses involved a generally weaker physical and psychological condition, you easily understand why the 80's is a precarious period in human life.

The transits of Uranus are probably the most remarkable. This is due to their uniqueness. Later in this book I will explain its influence in the Houses. For the time being, use the following list of aphorisms to get accustomed to the basic effect of the transiting aspects produced by Uranus with the other planets and elements in the chart.

Remember that the transit of a planet forming an aspect with another influences the basic energy of that planet and the areas represented by both transiting and radical planets (Houses belonging to the signs ruled by such planets) as well as the areas represented by the Houses where the planets are in the birth chart and where the transit occurs.

In the example chart on the following page, Uranus transits in House VII in Scorpio. It forms a square with natal Sun in House XI in Aquarius, a sign ruled by Uranus, while the Sun rules House IV in

Leo. Houses IV, VII and XI are affected by this transit as well as House VI, where Uranus is in the birth chart.

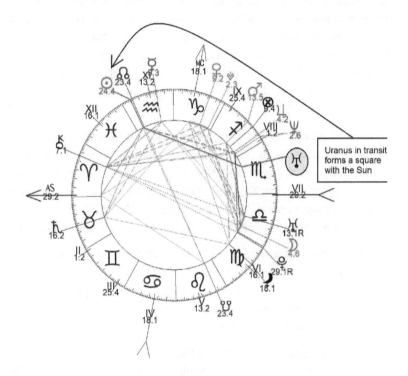

Uranus in transit forms a square with the Sun

The transiting aspects of Uranus

Uranus in harmony with the Sun

This long period is marked by an accrued adaptability and more originality to obtain better and quicker results in the areas represented by both Uranus and the Sun in the birth chart. Unexpected positive events, opportunities, and situations are likely to radically change life with a degree of satisfaction that depends on the natural ability to react quickly and positively to good surprises.

Uranus in dissonance with the Sun

Unexpected events are likely to produce various setbacks and errors due to a tendency to marginalised actions and reactions in the areas represented by the Sun and Uranus in the birth chart. Physical and psychological health condition may be affected by sudden functional changes and drops of vital energy. Relaxation and meditation are advised to counterbalance the disturbing influence of this transit.

Uranus in harmony with the Moon

Spontaneous expression of the emotions benefits personal and family relationships as well as the career especially if it requires important social contacts and dealings with people or the public. Uranus improves the energy and potential to succeed in the areas represented by the Houses in Aquarius (Uranus) and Cancer (Moon) in the birth chart, and by the Houses where Uranus is transiting.

Uranus in dissonance with the Moon

This transit produces a tendency to emotional instability due to sudden and unexpected events in the areas represented by the Houses in Aquarius and Cancer. Health may become a source of concerns due to emotional stress or hereditary conditions. The nervous system will benefit from relaxation and meditation sessions to counterbalance the disturbing influence of Uranus.

Uranus in harmony with Mercury

During this transit, intellectual adaptability, creativity and originality are greatly enhanced. Uranus favours communication and movement. It improves mental awareness and speed of comprehension. Extremely useful while studying, this transit is a source of renewed positive energy that promotes success from surprising opportunities in most unexpected areas.

Uranus in dissonance with Mercury

Various unexpected, troubling events are likely to temper the natural intellectual and mental potentials. Uranus increases instability in the areas represented by both planets in the chart. Focusing and concentrating on any subject for a long time becomes difficult and a source of misunderstanding and errors. A tendency to marginal behaviour is also indicated, with unpleasant consequences.

Uranus in harmony with Venus

Great changes are likely during this type of transit with important repercussions in love life and in areas where creativity is a valuable asset. Luck, providential events or encounters may also play an important role in the development of the areas represented by both planets in the chart. This transit is often marked by major changes of fate with surprisingly positive long-lasting consequences.

Uranus in dissonance with Venus

Unexpected and unwanted changes often occur during this type of transit. It may more particularly affect love life, friendship and the areas represented by the Houses in Aquarius and Taurus. Uranus produces a tendency to strive for freedom and independence excessively with detrimental long-term consequences such as marginalisation, health disorders and loss of self-esteem.

Uranus in harmony with Mars

During this type of transit, the ability to act and react quickly and efficiently is greatly enhanced with positive consequences in the areas of life represented by both planets in the chart. Originality of action and inventiveness produce most interesting results. These potentials are a spontaneous source of benefit during this period. Being different increases positive recognition and rewards.

Uranus in dissonance with Mars

Impatience and nervousness may link to aggressiveness and various incidents with their sudden and unpleasant consequences in the areas represented by the Houses in Aquarius and Aries in the chart. An effort is necessary to avoid speeding where circumstances impose to slow down. Not respecting the rhythm creates memorable discords, painful breakups, and various setbacks.

Uranus in harmony with Vesta
The ability to preserve harmony and balance is a quality that allows peaceful long-lasting success. Originality and inventiveness serve the potential to create and synchronize personal needs and desires to succeed in life, more particularly in the areas represented by both planets in the chart. Creative originality is enhanced. Unexpected positive changes are indicated in personal relationships, professional partnerships, or social encounters with uncommon individuals.

Uranus in dissonance with Vesta
Life is full of surprises, some of which have disrupting effects. During this transit, loss of balance is triggered by unexpected unpleasant events imposing major changes especially in the areas represented by the Houses in Aquarius and Libra in the birth chart. A greater need for freedom and independence in personal relationships may marginalise rather than stabilise.

Uranus in harmony with Jupiter
Good surprises and opportunities are more frequent during this type of transit. Uranus produces major changes that have positive and progressive influences in the areas represented by the Houses in Aquarius and Sagittarius in the birth chart. This beneficial transit has a tempering effect on other dissonant aspects produced by other transits. Strikes of luck are possible with exceptional consequences.

Uranus in dissonance with Jupiter
Taking risks in business with original but unpractical ideas are some of the consequences of this type of transit. Ambitions need to be addressed with patience and determination. Uranus indicates sudden changes of style, opinion, direction, and good fortune. These will be more remarkable in the areas represented by both planets in the chart. Blood pressure or hepatic disorders are also possible.

Uranus in harmony with Saturn

The past and the future cohabit and cooperate constructively during this type of transit. There is a greater potential to transform and reform the old to blend it with the new. Based on personal experience, positive changes can be organised and finalised with long-term consequences. These are more remarkable in the areas represented by both planets in the chart. Reforms become a source of success based on acquired knowledge and values to provide durable results.

Uranus in dissonance with Saturn

The past is threatened by unwanted changes of karmic nature in the areas represented by both planets in the chart. Life is made up of many surprises, some of which profoundly affect our daily routine and habits. They push us to challenge our inner potentials to adapt and gain rather than lose from difficulties. During this period, major existential doubts need to be dealt with as wisely as possible.

Uranus in harmony with Chiron

The ability to observe, analyse, and to focus on small details to understand the whole to which they belong is greatly enhanced during this type of transit. Uranus produces instant understanding and adaptability to physiological and existential changes with their psychological repercussions. The areas represented by both planets gain from unexpected events and situations in various ways.

Uranus in dissonance with Chiron

Sudden illnesses or changes in physiological conditions are likely during this type of transit. It affects the nervous system, digestion, and the organs and functions represented by the sign where Chiron is in the chart and the sign where Uranus transits. The areas of life linked to the Houses involved are likely to suffer various disruptions, especially if Chiron and Uranus are discordant in the birth chart.

Uranus in harmony with Uranus

This transit rare lasts for several years during which the ability to change, reform, adapt, and invent is a source of success in the areas represented by the House in Aquarius and the House where Uranus transits. The positive influence is useful to counterbalance other disturbing transits from other planets with other elements in the chart. Increased flexibility of thoughts and movements allows for quick reactivity to seize opportunities while avoiding unpleasant incidents.

Uranus in dissonance with Uranus
Uranus produces profound changes through its detrimental influence that challenge the ability to focus and act rationally. Reforms are an absolute must despite the lack of insurance of long-lasting success. The effect concerns the areas represented by the House in Aquarius and the House where Uranus transits. However, unexpected events encourage karmic and personal evolution.

Uranus in harmony with Neptune
This transit enhances intuition, creativity, and artistic inspiration. It combines the ability to feel with inventiveness and originality of mind and spirit. Unusual events are a source of philosophical and spiritual evolution. The areas represented by both planets in the chart are at the origin of the positive changes bestowed by Uranus. Unique and extraordinary encounters and situations are predictable.

Uranus in dissonance with Neptune
What we believe is not always a reflection of reality. During this kind of transit, it is absolutely necessary to concentrate on the rational side of life to avoid mistakes and their unpleasant consequences. Unstable hormonal function may cause health concerns. Uranus also affects the areas represented by the Houses in Aquarius and Pisces. Drastic changes of fortune are to be expected.

Uranus in harmony with Pluto
This transit increases the natural ability to regenerate. Less favourable influences occurring during the same period are dealt with more efficiently. A profound change of behaviour and needs is likely in the areas represented by both planets in the chart. The physical and psychological energy flow is stronger. It is a source of determined and positive action with long-lasting repercussions.

Uranus in dissonance with Pluto
Life can be tough and hazardous when this kind of transit occurs. There is a tendency to take unnecessary risks that may lead to

unpleasant and painful results. Too radical and expeditive, actions and reactions in critical situations become destructive. The areas represented by both planets are primarily concerned. Major events of a profound karmic nature are predictable.

Uranus in harmony with the Ascendant

This transit allows more flexibility and resilience to deal with various aspects of private life. Uranus enhances authenticity and adaptability in the areas it represents in the chart. The positive energy emanates from the House where Uranus transits as they become a source of inspiration to transform and reform intelligently. Major positive changes are therefore predictable during this transit.

Uranus in dissonance with the Ascendant

This type of transit tends to produce sudden changes of moods and behaviour. Unexpected events may be responsible for distressing challenges in the areas represented by the House in Aquarius stemming from the House where Uranus transits. Nervousness and impatience characterise the effect of this transit. It can also interfere with various physiological functions and affect the state of health.

Uranus in harmony with the Mid Heaven

Great changes are to be expected. Sudden events and opportunities have an extremely positive effect on the evolution of the career or the realisation of most important projects. It is a period of enhanced originality and inventiveness to favour long-lasting realisations. The motivating energy flow stems from the area represented by the House in Aquarius and the House where Uranus transits.

Uranus in dissonance with the Mid Heaven

Unexpected events strongly challenge social and professional status. Drastic changes may affect the whole career. Uranus makes it difficult to follow the rules and to stay in line with co-workers and hierarchy. Adaptability and reactivity are a must to fight adversity and restore balance. Unpleasant events are likely in the areas linked to the House in Aquarius and the House transited by Uranus.

Lesson 6

Neptune

Due to the very slow speed on its orbit around the Sun, Neptune is said to have a generational influence. This planet transits one full sign in fourteen years and the whole zodiac in 165 years. The role of Neptune in a birth chart in important. If it is a dominant planet, it often indicates some difficulty to address earthly realities, but it confers strong imagination, intuition, and creativity. Neptune evokes a more contemplative than rationally active aptitude.

The transits of Neptune in aspect with its own position in the chart are rare, but they last a long time. See the chart below showing the different aspects and the ages when they form. Note that the influence lasts some years before and after the exact aspect indicated in the chart.

Conjunction	Sextile	Square	Trine	Inconjunct	Opposition
Around 165	Around 27	Around 42	Around 55	Around 70	Around 82

A transiting aspect of Neptune can have a remarkable influence for many years. The basic effect is altered or dynamized by other transits occurring simultaneously. At 42, when Neptune forms a square with its original position, Uranus forms an opposition with its own position.

Both transiting aspects are collaborating to produce major changes and much confusion and inspiration. Mars plays a triggering role that needs to be taken into consideration. It makes a conjunction with Neptune up to seven time during its fourteen-year transit in a sign.

I consider a transiting aspect operational from the entry in a sign until the planet exits that same sign. It is of course much stronger when the aspect is exact. In Neptune's case, the influence of a transiting aspect can therefore last for up to fourteen years...

Neptune represents intuition, inspiration, feelings, the connexion with the invisible, the astral plans and the so-called "spiritual dimension". Neptune is also linked to confusion, mental and psychosomatic illness, and inner unrest. Neptune represents the soul and what it contains in terms of immaterial values, and beliefs that make it only partially in harmony with earthly reality.

A transit of Neptune in harmony with its own position (sextile or trine) enhances intuition and inspiration with their beneficial influence in the areas represented by the House in Pisces and the House where Neptune transits.

A similar effect is produced when Neptune forms harmonious transiting aspects with other elements in the chart. Its positive energy perdures for years, allowing great evolution by enhancing the ability to feel and to act accordingly especially when other beneficial transits occur simultaneously to support Neptune's influence. Neptune is a trans-saturnian "karmic planet".

Neptune can produce long periods of enhanced inspiration during which evolution depends on the ability to express our lofty nature to fulfill our dreams. When the aspect formed are dissonant, confusion and uncertainty prevail. They are however useful because they force us to call on higher plans of consciousness to avoid losing contact with earthly reality. To rely on it makes intuition stronger by the day, working like fog lights on our existential vehicle to avoid treacherous obstacles.

Neptune links us to our soul and invites us to freely and spontaneously express our subtle and sublime side to access the invisible world where magical encounters and wonderful discoveries can be made.

Let us now discuss the potential influence of Neptune when it forms transiting aspects with its own position in the chart. We will begin with the half sextile.

THE HALF SEXTILE

As you know now, Neptune is a slow, very slow, planet. This means that only one half sextile with its own position is possible in a lifetime. It occurs at 14 and can last until 28 years of age. It is an important period marked by the development of our personality, talents, potentials, and sensibility to the environment. Neptune instils our dreams into our heads. It is then up to us to realise them or not. Hopes and illusions are also represented by this planet. It is the link between Heaven and Earth. That is why Neptune makes us aware of the spiritual dimension to which we all belong.

The teenage period is filled with existential questions. The young ones are discoverers. They are more adventurous than many adults because they cannot evaluate the risks that they defy. It is a major moment in life in terms of aspirations and ambitions. New needs and new feelings emerge. Sensibility to the vibration of the outside world awakens latent potentials and talents, as well as fears and uncertainty. Creativity becomes a tool, a medium to express incomprehensible sensations. Emotional tsunamis are frequent. They increase vulnerability. The subtle plans of existence invite to a voyage of a lifetime. It a wonderful, but troubling period.

Because it can last as long as fourteen years, depending on other transiting aspects involving Neptune while forming a half sextile with its own position, the no-man's land thus created can be quite difficult to live. Daily reality too …

At most only 28 when the transiting half sextile ends, the evolution of consciousness has gone a long way. The young adult is not a child anymore, nor a teenager. If this first aspect of Neptune with own position is not "backed up" by other important harmonious transits it may become difficult to concretely gain from a fourteen-year experience of this kind. The next step being the sextile, at last, many dreams will have a chance to come true!

Although the half sextile is an uneasy period, it is an obligatory passage benefit from the beneficial sextile that follows. This one can also last for as much as fourteen years. Naturally, the exact aspect is the strongest. You need to check it out in the ephemeris to precisely determine its period of activity.

THE SEXTILE

Contrary to Jupiter, Saturn, Chiron and Uranus, Neptune can only form one transiting sextile with its own position. It precedes the transiting square. It allows to use the beneficial influence of this aspect to prepare for the long period of transiting square that I describe next in this chapter.

No matter what planet or element concerned, Neptune always act softly. Tensions, conflicts, and accidents are not directly due to Neptune's influence. Other transits (especially those of Mars) are needed to forecast this type of perturbation.

As a rule, the sextile enhances sensibility and intuition to benefit from the basic influence of the sextile. Inspiration is a source of success, wellbeing, and subtle satisfaction. It protects from the influence of unpleasant events. Enhanced sixth sense is useful to avoid incidents, errors, and accidents.

Neptune is a holistic revealer. It puts forward the link with the spiritual dimension of life. During the transiting sextile with it own position in my birth chart, between 1976 and 1977, I was initiated to astral travel through a book[9] by Robert Monroe.[10] I recommend this book if you are interested in discovering how astral travel can change your life and improve your awareness.

The exact sextile is at its highest level between the ages of 25 and 28. However, according to its original position in a chart, the exact

---

[9] https://www.monroeinstitute.org/products/monroe-robert-a-journeys-out-of-the-body
[10] https://www.monroeinstitute.org/pages/our-purpose

aspect happens earlier or later. For example, at 15° in a sign, the effect of the sextile begins at around 21 years of age. If it is positioned near the end of a sign, the influence can begin as young as 14 or 15 years of age. But the true aspect always occurs between 25 and 28 or even 30 years of age, depending on the orb allowed to the transiting sextile. It varies from 2° to 5°. Astrologers have different personal opinions about the orbs of radical and transiting aspects.

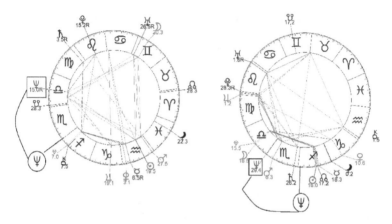

In the chart on the left, Neptune stands at 15° in Libra. It will take approximately 21 years for the planet to begin its transit in Sagittarius, and the sextile effect that will last for fourteen years.

In the chart on the right, Neptune stands at 29° in Libra. It will take only 14 years for Neptune to begin its transit in Sagittarius and the sextile effect that will last for about fourteen years.

In both instances, however, Neptune needs around 28 years to form an exact sextile with its own position.

Look in the ephemeris to precisely determine the moment when Neptune changes sign to begin its transiting sextile aspect with its own position.

THE SQUARE

A transiting sextile of Neptune slowly, but surely, leads to a square, an important configuration, the influence of which can perdure for as long as fourteen years. If it indicates a period of inner confusion, happily enough, we know that a transit never acts on its own. It is useful, for example, to consider the movements of Pluto because it often produces a sextile with Neptune. Pluto represents the potential to regenerate, to withstand difficulties, and to heal after an illness, or stand back up after a fall. Chapter 7 deals with Pluto.

The discordance of the square is derived from the elements of the signs involved in this configuration. As explained earlier in this book, Fire with Water, Earth with Air, and vice-versa, do not mix easily. The mix is more spontaneous and harmonious in the case of the sextile that blend Earth with Water, Fire with Air, and vice-versa.

When Neptune is not in accord with itself, the reality of life seems more confused and uncertain. A feeling of not being out of tune with life alters the potential to succeed concretely. Intuition is stronger but is not the positive guide it was during the period of the sextile. On the contrary, a tendency to believe blindly creates unrealisable dreams or unrealistic fears and apprehensions.

Disillusion and disappointment are likely due to lack of objectivity. Human relationships, health, career, and other important sectors of life are affected. The areas represented by Neptune (House in Pisces), by the House where Neptune is found in the birth chart, and the House where Neptune transits are primarily concerned.

Neptune act in an imperceptive manner, slowly and profoundly. Only one transiting square is possible during a human lifespan. During this long period, the more we think we are right, the more we disconnect from reality.

This transit is at its strongest at around 42 years of age, when Uranus forms an opposition with its own position (as seen in chapter 5). The major changes occurring at that age are bound to be a source of confusion and uncertainty.

The influence of the transiting square of Neptune with its own position can begin much earlier than 42. It partly explains the role of Uranus in terms of the major changes it often indicates. As explained about the sextile, if Neptune is positioned at the end of a sign, its influence is felt up to fourteen years before the exact aspect. If it is positioned in the first few degrees of a sign, the exact square reaches a climax as soon as Neptune enters the sign in which it will be active for fourteen years.

THE TRINE

As seen earlier in this book, the planets in transit form two types of trine with their own position. The first one leads to an inconjunct and the second one to a square. Both aspects being somewhat dissonant, they announce more hustle and strife than effortless accomplishment.

In Neptune's case, only one trine is possible. It is at its strongest at 56 years of age, although its influence perdures as long as the transit in the sign concerned.

Lack of objectivity is one the main consequence of a discordant transit of Neptune with its own position. That is why it is important to derive as much benefit as possible from the transiting trine to give the soul a better grip on earthly matters to deal with the reality of life in a lofty, yet efficient manner. Neptune enhances spontaneous inspiration and its positive influence to favour intuitive and creative realisations.

The period of transiting inconjunct that follows is comparable to being navigating on the ocean of life in a rudderless boat. However, what has been achieved during the period of transiting trine can positively compensate the elements of confusion emanating from the inconjunct. There is tendency to dream passively rather than to act spontaneously.

It is therefore important to get as much done on the highest level as possible during the period of transiting trine to deserve to relax and enjoy the good results while transiting Neptune forms an inconjunct with its own position.

THE INCONJUNCT AND THE OPPOSITION

Knowing that Neptune takes 165 years to complete a full circle around the zodiac, it forms an inconjunct, then an opposition with itself at 70, then 82 or 83 years of age. Meanwhile, Uranus is about to come back to its original position in the chart for the first time. Pluto is also nearing the opposition with itself. Three major cosmic events occurring simultaneously for the first time in someone's life are bound to produce major reactions. It the opposition frees Neptune from its latent influence, which can be the moment the soul (Neptune) chooses to free itself from the body and thus get prepared for a future incarnation, the period of inconjunct is made up of all sorts of petty ailments that can become more invasive without proper care. In any case, the event is likely to produce various reactions that may greatly destabilise and threaten both physical and psychological life potentials.

The opposition of a planet to itself is comparable to the effect of a mirror. The action of reflecting a reversed image highlights imperfections and other flaws in the areas represented by that planet in the birth chart. During this type of transit, life is calling on us to take a look at reality. Just like Uranus and Pluto, Neptune only creates one opposition with itself in a lifetime. Its effect spans over a number of years, due to the slow speed of the planet around the zodiac.

In my opinion, the opposition of Neptune with itself puts forward the higher spiritual reality of life. This is perceived consciously or unconsciously, but it is strong. It is like a call from heaven. Heard or not, when we reach the noble age of 80 years and more, we understand that our existential journey is not far from reaching its final destination.

During this transit, Neptune passes through the opposite sign and opposite House to that in which it is found in the birth chart. Opposite signs and Houses are complementary. Hence, Neptune may also show how to behave in order to conciliate our contradictions to adopt a more compassionate approach to the areas represented by such opposed Houses, while striving to blend the energies of the opposite signs.

You will see in the list of aphorisms included in this chapter how Neptune acts on the other objects and elements of the chart during its peripli around the zodiac. The opposition provides a subtle access to the loftier meaning of the element concerned and the areas it represents in the chart. Neptune accentuates the ability to feel and to connect with the principle linked to the planet involved to gain valuable repercussions in the areas represented.

THE CONUNCTION

Neptune will not return to its original position during a human lifespan, unless the person lives to be at least 165 years old... Nevertheless, from a historical point of view, could this cosmic event create a resonance with what happened when Neptune was at the same position around the zodiac 165 years before your birth? It may be interesting to find out. You may have an ancestor born that year with whom you may bear intriguing resemblance...

In 1848, for example, Neptune was beginning its long transit in Pisces. We can imagine that it has an important effect on idealistic perception and needs of peoples and societies. The site Wikipedia.com gives this information:

*The **Revolutions of 1848**, known in some countries as the **Springtime of the Peoples** or the **Spring of Nations**, were a series of political upheavals throughout Europe in 1848. It remains the most widespread revolutionary wave in European history.*

The revolutions were essentially democratic and liberal in nature, with the aim of removing the old monarchical structures and creating independent nation-states. The revolutions spread across Europe after an initial revolution began in France in February. Over 50 countries were affected, but with no significant coordination or cooperation among their respective revolutionaries. Some of the major contributing factors were widespread dissatisfaction with political leadership, demands for more participation in government and democracy, demands for freedom of the press, other demands made by the working class, the upsurge of nationalism, the regrouping of established government forces, and the European Potato Failure, which triggered mass starvation, migration, and civil unrest.

The uprisings were led by temporary coalitions of reformers, the middle classes ("the bourgeoisie") and workers. However, the coalitions did not last long. Many of the revolutions were quickly suppressed; tens of thousands of people were killed, and many more were forced into exile. Significant lasting reforms included the abolition of serfdom in Austria and Hungary, the end of absolute monarchy in Denmark, and the introduction of representative democracy in the Netherlands. The revolutions were most important in France, the Netherlands, Italy, the Austrian Empire, and the states of the German Confederation that would make up the German Empire in the late 19th and early 20th century.

This article is a reflexion of the situation in the world 165 years later, since 2012. We deplored so many riots, demonstrations, and revolutions in many countries where people became hostile to their leaders with a strong determination to overthrow their regime.

The Catholic Church was involved in many scandals that had a detrimental effect on its spiritual aura. In 2019, Jupiter transited in Sagittarius, its sign of rulership. It formed a discordant aspect (square) with Neptune, also in its sign of rulership. The law intervened and much was officially done in an attempt to repair the damages. At last, the Church recognised its errors, coverups, and other silencing of the truth for so many years.

As seen earlier, Neptune began its transit in Pisces in 2012 (February). What happened then to the Church? On Wikipedia's website I found the following interesting information:

In the « Motu Proprio » [11] *(Porta Fidei) the Pope Benoit XVI announced a year of faith. It began on October 11, 2012 to*

---

[11] In law, **motu proprio** (Latin for: "on his own impulse") describes an official act taken without a formal request from another party. Some jurisdictions use the term *"sua sponte"* for the same concept.

commemorate the fiftieth anniversary of the opening of the Vatican II Council. It ended on November 24, 2013. The Pope retired on February 28, 2013 at 20:00 (8:00 PM). His reason for taking this decision was quite confused...

On that day, the Sun formed a conjunction with Neptune in Pisces, together with other planets transiting in this sign. Benoit XVI chose a time to coincide precisely with beneficial aspects formed with the planetary "congregation" in Pisces, more especially a trine with the Mid-Heaven and Saturn that you can see in the chart of the event reproduced below.

Abdication Benoit XVI 28/02/2013 20:00 Rome, Italy

Comparing this chart to the Pope's birth chart reproduced on the following page, we can imagine why he chose this particular time of the day to abdicate in the best possible configuration and I do not believe one second that it was pure coincidence...

Benoit XVI   16/04/1927 04:15 Marktl, Germany

At the time chosen to abdicate, the Sun was conjunct the Pope's Ascendant, and the Ascendant of the day was conjunct his Lilith in Libra, while the Moon was about to form a conjunction with its own position in Benoit XVI's birth chart at 17° in Libra. See if other transits attract your attention. Jupiter and Saturn were quite interesting too. Nothing is coincidental…

Neptune and the other elements in the chart

The transiting conjunctions of Neptune with other elements of the chart are to be analysed two ways.

One is to consider that the Neptunian energy enhances intuition, extrasensory perceptions, sensibility to non-material aspects of a situation in the areas represented by the elements and Houses concerned.

The other one is linked to the fact that Neptune tends to be responsible for long periods of inner confusion, uncertainty and feelings of inadequacy to deal with realities inherent to the areas represented by the elements and Houses concerned.

What are the elements and Houses concerned?

Observe the chart below and you will easily understand.

Neptune is transiting the conjunction Sun/Venus in Aquarius in House I (Ascendant). The transit concerns this House and two others; those represented by the Sun and Venus (Houses VII and IV). It also affects the person's love-life (Venus) and physical energy (Sun). Neptune also enhances the influences of the other aspects involving the Sun and Venus with the Moon (square), Uranus (trine) and Pluto (opposition).

See the list of aphorisms next to familiarise yourself with the possible influence of Neptune in transiting aspects with the various elements of a birth chart.

The transiting aspects of Neptune

Neptune in harmony with the Sun

This period will be marked by an increase of the ability to connect with the invisible and the spiritual sides of life. More intuition and self-awareness make it easier to benefit from many opportunities instinctively and spontaneously. This type of transit is also useful to counteract less favourable influences from other slow planets. The areas represented by the Houses ruled by the Sun and Neptune, and the House where Neptune transits are primarily concerned.

Neptune in dissonance with the Sun

This transit may produce confusion and uncertainty about self-image and social positioning. Personal projects and/or career are subject to doubts and inconsistency. A tendency to believe rather than verify rationally is a source of errors and disappointment. This influence of Neptune primarily concerns the areas of life represented by the Houses in Leo (Sun) and Pisces (Neptune) and by the Houses where Neptune transits.

Neptune in harmony with the Moon

This type of transit is likely to enhance the creative potential and the need to improve intuition and sixth sense to the point of bestowing clairvoyance ability with positive incidence on artistic creativity or family situation. Enjoyment may be more particularly significant in the areas represented by the Houses in Cancer (Moon) and Pisces (Neptune), and by the House where Neptune transits.

Neptune in dissonance with the Moon

During this long period, Neptune is likely to enhance emotivity and vulnerability to imagination and inner confusion. Uncertainty may be a source of errors in the areas represented by the Houses in Cancer (Moon) and Pisces (Neptune), and by the House where Neptune transits. Neptune can also affect the hormonal function or trigger allergic reactions and psychosomatic disorders.

Neptune in harmony with Mercury

This type of transit increases intuition and intellectual sensibility and creativity. It produces more spontaneous connexion with the spiritual dimension and favours greater awareness of the self in accordance with to the need of the soul. Neptune plays a major role to improve intellectual understanding and communication. The areas of life represented by the Houses in Gemini (Mercury) and Pisces (Neptune) and where Neptune transits are primarily concerned.

Neptune in dissonance with Mercury

During this long period, the tendency to believe rather than verify rationally is like to be a source of errors, setbacks, and uncertainty. Neptune enhances the role of imagination that confers a deformed perception of reality. It is more remarkable in the areas represented by the Houses in Gemini (Mercury) and Pisces (Neptune), and where Neptune is transiting.

Neptune in harmony with Venus

This type of transit is particularly favourable to artists who benefit from increased inspiration due to a more spontaneous link with higher levels of consciousness where sensitive minds become canal for pure creativity. Love life may also be improved, as well as the procreation potentials. Strikes of luck are also indicated in the areas represented by the Houses in Taurus (Venus) and Pisces (Neptune), and where Neptune is transiting.

Neptune in dissonance with Venus

This period is likely to be marked by sentimental disappointment due to a tendency to believe rather than to rely on verified rational facts. The need for love and approbation increases dependency on the other person and creates a distorted understanding of the situation and relationship. The areas represented by the Houses in Taurus (Venus) and Pisces (Neptune), and where Neptune is transiting are primarily concerned. The reproductive organs, the skin and the thyroid function may be affected during this long transit of Neptune.

Neptune in harmony with Mars

This transit enhances the natural potential to fight for the higher principles of life. Intuitive reactions and imaginative actions favour success. Instinctively knowing what to do and when to do it is a valuable asset to obtain better results. The areas represented by the Houses in Aries (Mars) and Pisces (Neptune), and where Neptune transits are primarily concerned.

Neptune in dissonance with Mars

During this long period, Neptune becomes a source of confusion and uncertainty that affects the ability to act and react efficiently. Imagination and beliefs produce instability and a tendency to behave according to unrealistic motivations. The areas represented by the Houses in Aries (Mars) and Pisces (Neptune), and where Neptune transits are primarily concerned.

Neptune in harmony with Vesta

This transit enhances creativity and the ability to preserve and restore balance and harmony instinctively, thanks to intuition and a better connexion with the subtle energy of life. Such qualities are useful to obtain better results in the areas represented by the Houses in Libra (Vesta) and Pisces (Neptune), and where Neptune transits. The beneficial influence of Neptune is also valuable to maintain optimum health condition.

Neptune in dissonance with Vesta

During this period, a tendency to feel insecure and easily destabilised is issued from beliefs and thoughts stemming from imaginary rather than rational sources. Loss of balance may be more particularly remarked in the areas represented by the Houses in Libra (Vesta) and Pisces (Neptune), and where Neptune is transiting. This transit is also known to create health concerns and psychosomatic disorders.

Neptune in harmony with Jupiter

This transit is a strong source of positive spiritual influence that enhances the ability to feel and to philosophically deal with the most important and sensitive subjects. Strikes of luck and extra ordinary opportunities are often responsible for major advancements in the areas represented by the Houses in Sagittarius (Jupiter) and Pisces (Pisces), and where Neptune is transiting.

Neptune in dissonance with Jupiter

During this period, Neptune creates a tendency to believe in unrealistic schemes and projects, with ambitions that surpass personal capacities in the areas represented by the Houses in Sagittarius (Jupiter) and Pisces (Neptune), and where Neptune is transiting. Blood pressure and circulation in the legs and feet may be sources of health concerns. Exaggerated symptoms can increase physical and psychological unwellness.

Neptune in harmony with Saturn

This transit allows for more intuition to favour concrete realisation of various projects. It tends to blend dream with reality and gives personal experience a more tangible influence on imagination and creativity. The areas represented by the Houses in Capricorn (Saturn) and Pisces (Neptune), and where Neptune transits are primarily concerned. Neptune is also useful to deal with hardship in a loftier and more efficient manner.

Neptune in dissonance with Saturn

During this type of transit renewed effort is necessary to tackle reality with more objectivity to avoid mistakes stemming from a tendency to dream and hope, but not to act accordingly. Confusion and a degree of uncertainty to deal with various obstacles and difficulties temper the ability to achieve important goals adequately. The areas represented by the Houses in Capricorn (Saturn) and Pisces (Neptune), and where Neptune transits are primarily concerned.

Neptune in harmony with Chiron

This transit has a positive influence on both physical and psychological health conditions. A positive link between the rational methodology to medicine and the holistic approach makes it possible to preserve or restore optimum capacities. Intuition is useful to connect with the higher meanings of difficulties, understanding subtle warnings and find adequate solutions. This is primarily observed in the areas represented by the Houses in Virgo (Chiron) and Pisces (Neptune) and where Neptune is transiting.

Neptune in dissonance with Chiron

During this long period, Neptune is likely to create confusion and uncertainty surrounding health and the necessary approach to preserve or restore optimum wellbeing. A tendency to imagine the worse rather than concentrate on the best, irrationally increases punctual and chronic disorders. The areas represented by the Houses in Virgo (Chiron) and Pisces (Neptune) and where Neptune is transiting are primarily concerned.

Neptune in harmony with Uranus

This transit enhances both imagination and inventiveness. It increases the ability to adapt quickly to life's circumstances and swiftly benefit from the most unexpected opportunities. Intellectual creativity is enhanced by greater intuition so useful to obtain better results and improve life in many ways. The areas represented by the Houses in Aquarius (Uranus) and Pisces (Neptune), and where Neptune is transiting, are primarily concerned.

Neptune in dissonance with Uranus

Imagination is a source of confusion and uncertainty that makes it more difficult to rationally deal with sudden changes. This transit may affect health through nervous system instability and hormonal imbalance. Social life may also become ambiguous and unpleasant. The areas represented by the Houses in Aquarius (Uranus) and Pisces (Neptune), and where Neptune is transiting, are primarily concerned.

Neptune in harmony with Neptune

This transit indicates a period of spiritual development and increase in creativity and imagination. The intuition is likely to be a source of extra ordinary experiences of a positive karmic nature. See what is explained in this chapter about the sextile and trine, the only two possible beneficial transiting aspect of Neptune with its own position in the chart. The areas represented by the House in Pisces and the House where Neptune is transiting are primarily concerned.

Neptune in dissonance with Neptune

During this long type of transit (only one square and one inconjunct are possible) a tendency to daydreaming is likely to affect the ability to concretely act and obtain concrete results. A feeling of uncertainty adds to the confusion without providing any rational solution. The areas represented by the House in Pisces and the House where Neptune is transiting, are primarily concerned.

Neptune in harmony with Pluto

This transit creates a natural connexion with the deeper meaning of life and death in a loftier and more spiritual manner. Neptune makes it easier to regenerate in case of illness or other existential difficulties. The ability to accept the principle of existential cycles helps manage losses and setbacks more philosophically. The areas represented by the Houses in Scorpio (Pluto) and Pisces (Neptune), and where Neptune is transiting, are primarily concerned.

Neptune in dissonance with Pluto

During this long period, the idea of death becomes a source of inner uncertainty and confusion. This may be due to a painful loss of someone close or to existential difficulties of a karmic nature. The soul is both attracted and frightened by the darkness. What needs to be destroyed, abandoned, or ended produces inner turmoil with unpleasant repercussions in the areas represented by the Houses in Scorpio (Pluto) and Pisces (Neptune), and the House where Neptune is transiting.

Neptune in harmony with the Ascendant

This transit enhances the intuitive relation between the higher realms of life and the inner self. More understanding of personal needs and qualities makes it easier to obtain better results in various situations. Creativity and imagination favour many aspects of existence. The areas represented by the House in Pisces and the House where Neptune transits primarily benefit from this positive influence.

Neptune in dissonance with the Ascendant

During this long period, it seems difficult to rationally connect with the self. Neptune increases uncertainty and confusion, while a tendency to believe rather than establish rational facts contributes to unpleasant mistakes and disappointment. The areas represented by the House in Pisces and the House where Neptune transits are primarily affected.

Neptune in harmony with the Mid-Heaven

Greater intuition and imagination increase the potential to succeed in realising important projects. A loftier approach to life's circumstances, makes it easier to deal with authority and hierarchy that contribute to better results in accordance with personal ambitions. Creativity may also become a complementary source of social satisfaction. The areas represented by the House in Pisces and the House where Neptune transits primarily benefit from this positive influence.

Neptune in dissonance with the Mid-Heaven

What we dream of achieving is not always rational enough to favour concrete positive results. This transit shows how much effort is necessary to remain as down-to-earth as possible to avoid mistakes and social or professional disappointment. It is advised not to build on unsure grounds and to take time to analyse all aspects of a proposition, contract or deal before engaging officially or legally. The areas represented by the House in Pisces and the House where Neptune transits are primarily affected.

Lesson 7

PLUTO

Alike Neptune's, Pluto's influence is generational. It represents the regeneration potential and the ability to question, destroy or transform to build or rebuild in accordance with a profound process of renovation that can take a few decades to accomplish. During Pluto's transits, the energy of the god of death is more remarkable in the areas represented by the House in Scorpio, the House where it is found in the chart and the House transited.

Pluto is the last planet of the solar system. It is also the farthest, with an average distance to the Sun of five billion kilometres. Not so long ago, Pluto was reduced to the rank of asteroid by the astronomical society. Later, a observation craft sent by NASA demonstrated that Pluto was a real planet with five natural satellites (moons). They were names Charon, Nix, Hydra, Styx, and Kerberos. With a 2.372 kilometres diameter, Pluto is the largest of the so-called "dwarf" planets. It takes Pluto 247 years and around 8 months to complete its orbit around the Sun. It turns on its axis in 6 days 9 hours 17 minutes precisely.

In Roman mythology, Pluto is the god of death, the guardian of hell who leads the dead into the other world. In Grecque mythology, its name is Hades.

In astrology, being the farthest planet to the Sun giver of life, Pluto represents death. However, oriental culture having introduced the principle of reincarnation, death becomes a passage leading to another life, which granted Pluto the status of regenerator rather than terminator…

In a birth chart, Pluto represents the potential to regenerate, to heal and recover from illness, setbacks, mistakes, and other "calamities".

It also represents endurance, determination, resistance, and resilience.

Although they can last for many years, the transits of Pluto have a unique in-depth influence because all aspects formed with the rest of the chart are a once in a lifetime occurrence.

Major and extraordinary periods of profound transformation happen while Pluto forms transiting aspects with its own position in the chart. The eccentric orbit of this planet makes it impossible to draw a chart of the transiting aspects formed with its own position. You need to refer to the ephemeris to find out.

I remind you that a transiting planet never acts alone. Transiting aspects must be analysed simultaneously rather than independently. The easiest way to do it is to draw the symbols of the slow planets around the chart, then check all possible aspects between them and with the rest of the chart. This process allows to get a more balanced appreciation of the transits.

The transits of Pluto affect a great number of people in the same areas of life in relation to other slow transiting planets such as Neptune and Uranus. These major configurations create sociological tendencies that are very interesting to observe and analyse in world astrology.

Pluto's influence is known to be quite destructive. The planet was discovered quite recently, in 1930, but it quickly became obvious to associate it to its given name of the god of death and reincarnation (regeneration).

Although very far from the Earth, this very small planet seems to have considerable influence, probably due to its extremely slow speed and a particular magnetic field that penetrates deep into life forms on Earth.

During the harmonious transiting aspects formed with its own position and with other elements in the chart, Pluto is known to increase regenerative potential, resilience and determination in the areas represented by the House transited by Pluto and those represented by the other planets involved.

During discordant transits, on the contrary, Pluto enhances destructive and self-destructive tendencies that can affect in various ways, both physically and psychologically, socially, privately, and professionally, depending on the chart, the elements, and the Houses concerned.

With Pluto, it is not about ending as such, but rather about phases and stages leading to a new birth or a new start. Death is just a passage to another life...

THE CONJUNCTION

No conjunction is possible between Pluto and its own position in the chart during the course of human lifetime. The planet takes about 248 years to come back to complete its orbit around the zodiac. Like Uranus and Neptune, Pluto's conjunctions with itself are however very interesting in world astrology.

On 20th November 2024, Pluto will begin a transit of almost twenty years in Aquarius. It will last until 20th January 2044.

The preceding occurrence dates back to 28th January 1778 and lasted until 27th December 1798. We know that during this historical period, people in various countries were so angry about their leaders, that it gradually led them to revolutions. In America, the conflict lasted 8 years, between 19th April 1775 and 3rd September 1783. America obtained its independence from the British Crown and became the USA on 4th July 1776 (Independence Day). The French revolution overthrew the monarchy on 14th July 1789. There was also a revolution in Belgium between 1789 and 1795; one in Russia between 1773 and 1775; and there was one in Poland in 1794...

Before Aquarius, Pluto has to transit through in Capricorn, where it is since 2008. The crash of the world economy following the financial scandal of the subprime.[12] This crisis was suppose to open up to a new world economy, but this dream did not become a reality.

Pluto acting in Capricorn is there to destroy dictatures and authoritarian regimes. Money being the "superior in chief", it became the target of much questioning and revisiting. The revolt of the Egyptians against their leader in 2010 started a wave of protest across the world in countries where people were oppressed by their governments. The growing dissatisfaction and bitterness among the people could very well lead to another period of destruction, rebellion, and revolution. 2020 was a crucial year that I foresaw and described in a video posted on my YouTube channel in July 2019. Jupiter, Saturn, and Pluto formed a unique conjunction in Capricorn, so rare that the last occurrence dated back 6,594 years before 2020, in 4,574 BC!

Some years later, in 2024, Pluto will begin its twenty-year transit in Aquarius. Is it going to produce similar situations as what happened in the late eighteenth century? It is unfortunately not impossible at all …

In a birth chart, the transits of Pluto forming conjunctions with other elements indicate periods of profound regeneration of the life principle represented by the element concerned (planet, House, and other objects). Regeneration is also remarked in the area represented by the House where Pluto transits. The notion of destruction in view of reconstruction is greatly emphasised. It is a very slow process. In one year, Pluto moves by one or two degrees around the zodiac. The areas of life concerned are submitted to a long period of "in-depth cleaning or detailing"… The necessity imposes itself gradually and becomes active when a faster transit passes by. "*Dying to be born again*" is Pluto's moto.

---

[12] **Subprime** refers to borrowers or loans, usually offered at rates well above the prime rate, that have poor credit ratings. **Subprime** lending is higher risk, given the lower credit rating of borrowers, and has in the past contributed to financial crises such as in 2008.

THE HALF SEXTILE

Depending on the year of birth, the exact transiting sextile form by Pluto with its own position in the chart, can happen at 12 years of age (natal Pluto in Scorpio or Sagittarius) or at 24 years of age (natal Pluto in Cancer or Leo). For a person born in July 1916, for example, the half sextile occurred in September 1940, 24 years later. For a person born in 1986, this same aspect occurred in June 1998, only twelve years later. The eccentric orbit of Pluto is responsible for such differences.

As explained earlier, the half sextile links planets or other elements that are in following signs. They are not compatible signs. The associations Fire-Earth, Air-Water, Fire-Water, and Air-Earth are not spontaneously blending. Hence, the energy emanating from their association is not harmonious, but discordant.

The period during which Pluto forms a half-sextile with its natal position, or with other elements in the chart, would therefore be marked by various setbacks and difficulties in the areas represented by the Houses concerned.

The effect is even stronger the semi sextile "cohabits" with a transit of Saturn in opposition with its natal position at 14 and 15 years of age. It is the case for people born with Pluto in Leo, although these transiting aspects are felt differently from one person to another.

When the half sextile occurs at 24 years of age, the person is an adult, responsible and supposedly balanced. The troubling influence of Pluto can then become more destructive. The questioning about the true value of life is more incisive, both personally and socially.

See how old you were when Pluto formed a half sextile with its own position in your chart. What do you remember from this period? Was it a happy moment of your life or a rather complicated one? If you have children, it may be useful to have a look at their chart to understand how and why Pluto has or had this type of influence because of this aspect.

If the exact aspect can be dated rather precisely, its influence can perdure for quite some time. It begins long before the exact aspect and continues on many months, even years, after. During this period, other transits may simultaneously support the troubling influence of Pluto to make it more demanding and complicated ...

THE SEXTILE

Once again, you need to consult the ephemerides to precisely determine the period during which Pluto formed a sextile with its own position in a chart. Although the exact ones is naturally more influent, all the aspects produced by Pluto are growing in strength long before the perfect aspect and perdure long after.

The transiting sextile with its own position tends to enhance the natural capacity to regenerate and to deal with the difficulties of life. It renders more determined and tenacious. According to the situation during this type of transit, Pluto allows greater potential to impose oneself, to rebound from setbacks, and to overtake various obstacles more efficiently.

Pluto's influence begins as soon as the planet enters into the sign concerned. The climax is reached when the aspect is exact (60° for the sextile). The role of the aspect of Pluto with its own position perdure for a very long time, for a few years. This is due to its slow speed of rotation around the zodiac and to the retrogradations.

Pluto's sextile with its own position, varies greatly, as explained earlier. Here are some examples for the sextile:

Pluto in Leo at birth produces a sextile with its own position that reaches its highest level (exact aspect) when the person is around 32 years of age.

Pluto in Libra at birth produces a sextile with its own position that reaches its highest level (exact aspect) when the person is around 24 years of age.

Pluto in Capricorn at birth produces a sextile with its own position that reaches its highest level (exact aspect) when the person is around 39 years of age.

You can imagine how different it is in the case of a square or a trine that will be delt with next. That is why you need the ephemerides to find the period during which the aspect is fully operational.

The sextile precedes a long period marked by a square. That is why the sextile needs to be taken full advantage of to be able to sustain the years of dissonance between transiting Pluto and its own position in the chart. *What goes up, must come down…*

The sextiles between transiting Pluto and other elements in the chart, increase the ability to deal with the areas represented by the elements concerned (planets, Houses, etc.) Use the list of aphorisms included in this chapter to inspire your analyses of this harmonic aspect that can prove very beneficial indeed.

THE SQUARE

Similar to the half sextile, the discordance produced by a square comes from the antagonism between Fire and Water, Air and Earth, Earth and Fire, and Water and Air. Although coexisting on our planet, contrary to air and fire immediately compatible, air and water share their atomic constitutions but if you want to mix them together you will find that it is not so easy…

When Pluto forms a square aspect with its natal position in the chart, all sorts of profound transformations take place gradually month after month and year after year. The consequences are often very serious in accordance with the overall tendency of the chart. Pluto is death. As such, it represents what must end. No one is immortal. Nothing lasts forever. Nothing is completely ours, all we possess is lent to us until we die.

From time to time it is essential to be able to accept fatality, the law of the cycles of life allows a more philosophical approach to the implacable power of death. The notion of destruction associated to Pluto has a definitive and unavoidable connotation. It becomes evident when a natural catastrophe destroys a city or a whole region. When this planet forms a discordant aspect with its own position or with other elements in the chart, the abilities to resist, to regenerate, to heal and to resist become essential assets to come out of the ordeal unharmed.

The square is at its strongest point when the angle between the elements concerned reaches 90°. With Pluto in Leo, for example, the effect of the square with its own position is strong between 44 and 45 years of age. With Pluto in Libra, the square occurs earlier, at around 37 years of age. Drastic changes with deep and long-lasting repercussions are also occurring when Pluto forms a square with any element in the chart, in the areas represented by the Houses concerned.

THE TRINE

The trine is beneficial because it has a deep regenerating influence that allows for much to be achieved while it lasts. The trine involves spontaneously compatible signs that belong to the same element (Fire, Earth, Air and Water). Pluto transiting a Fire sign is in perfect relationship with anything positioned in one or both of the other Fire signs. The same applies to the Earth, Air and Water signs.

Pluto positioned in a Fire sign has a flamboyant influence. Its destructive energy expresses itself suddenly, vehemently, even violently. Creativity and sentiments feed the regenerating capacity and colour the existence with panache.

Pluto positioned in an Earth sign has a down-to-Earth influence that enhances the regenerating potential in areas linked to the material side of life. The need to succeed financially is often a source of renewed motivation and sustained determination.

Pluto positioned in an Air sign has a cerebral influence that enhances the ability to philosophically deal with the realities of life. The need to succeed academically feeds the ability to consider profound transformations necessary on all levels of consciousness.

Pluto positioned in a Water sign acts on the emotions and sensibility. The need for profound transformations of moral values is enhanced. It indicates tenacity and determination to deal with situations and projects involving the family and the country.

The transiting trine formed by Pluton with its own position in the chart happens only once in a human lifetime. It lasts for many years, thus allowing greater regeneration and higher level realisations. As soon as Pluto enters into the sign forming a trine with the sign where it was at birth, the energy of the aspect begins to act. In some cases, the positive influence can perdure around twenty years, until Pluto transits into the following sign.

Examples:

1 - Pluto found at 1° in Leo in a chart begins to form a trine with its own position when it enters in Sagittarius at about 57 years of age. The effect lasts until the end of the transit in Sagittarius, when the person is around 69 years of age.

2 - Pluto found at 29° in Leo, the effect of the trine begins much earlier, when it begins the transit in Sagittarius at around 39 years of age to last until the person is around 51 years of age.

Once again, it is necessary to check in the ephemerides to precisely determine the beginning and the end of a period of transiting trine, knowing that the climax is always reached when the aspect is as close as possible to 120° (trine).

Enhanced regenerating capacity becomes a true source of revitalization. No matter what happens (within reasonable limits) strength and determination unite to allow various forms of revival, healing, and recovery more likely to involve and favour the areas represented by the House in Scorpio and the House where Pluto transits.

As explained earlier, Pluto is the slowest planet of the solar system and its orbit is eccentric. It is not possible to determine the age of such a transit without consulting the ephemerides to find the years during which this positive influence is operational.

Two examples:

1 - For a person born in the 1940's with Pluto in Leo, the transiting trine with its own position occurs in 1995 when Pluto is in Sagittarius at around 55 years of age.

2 - For a person born in 1995 with Pluto in Sagittarius benefits from the transiting trine with its own position in 2068 when Pluto is in Aries, at about 73 years of age…

THE INCONJUNCT

The inconjunct precedes the opposition. It occurs at an older age. When transiting Pluto forms an inconjunct with its own position in the chart, all sorts of disturbances and existential disorders are to be deplored. The effect can last for some years as it is strong when the angle is between 145 and 155 degrees. Pluto may take up to seven to eight years to transit those ten degrees.

The inconjunct involves incompatible signs in a similar manner with the semi sextile and the square: Fire with Water, Earth with Air, Water with Air, and Fire with Earth.

The initial position of Pluto in a chart reveals quite a lot about the end of life. The baby-boom generation is particularly suffering from heart diseases. Pluto is in Leo, the sign of the Sun that also represents the heart in medical astrology. The Sun is also associated with the eyes and the vision.

Pluto in Fire signs supposes a rather quick and often violent end of life. It is a strong position that can turn around to become more threatening than protecting. Does it mean that with Pluto in a Fire sign life expectancy is shorter than with Pluto in a Water or Earth sign? I cannot answer this question because I have not done any research or statistics on the subject.

What I have mostly verified is that the position of Pluto depends more on the rest of the chart and on the types of aspects in which it is involved that on the element of the sign in which it stands.

However, when Pluto is in discordance with itself during a transit around the zodiac, the resistance to existential stress is less effective. More vulnerability to infections and to other threatening ailments can become a source of greater concern, especially at an older age. The long period of inconjunct could be compared to the preparation phase to the "great voyage".

Three examples:

1 - A person born with Pluto in Leo begins to feel the effect of the inconjunct around the age of 65, when it transits in Capricorn, although the influence can perdure until 74 or 75 years of age.

2 - A person born with Pluto in Virgo begins to feel the effect of the inconjunct goes through a similar phase at around the same age as the person with Pluto in Leo.

3 - A person born in 1972 with Pluto Libra, however, will be impacted by the transiting inconjunct with its own position in the chart in 2044, at around 72 years of age, but the transit in Pisces will last almost 20 years…

Besides its influence on health and vitality, the inconjunct announces a period of major transformation in the areas represented by the House in Scorpio, the House in which Pluto is found in the chart, and the House where it is transiting.

THE OPPOSITION

The opposition formed by transiting Pluto with its own position in the chart is a unique event that many do not live long enough to witness. Depending on the sign position at birth, it can take up to 124 years to occur.

Two examples:

1 - Someone born with Pluto at 0° Cancer in 1913, needs to live until 2008/2009 to reach the glorious age of 95 or 96 for the transiting opposition to occur.

2 - Someone born in 1949, with Pluto in Leo, a transiting opposition is formed when Pluto transits in Aquarius from 2024 onwards, at 75 years of age.

The opposition is likely to confirm the detrimental effect of the inconjunct if nothing is done to counteract the influence of Pluto. Knowing that Pluto represents the capacity to regenerate, while opposing itself, this potential tends to get weaker and less protective of the general state of health. The body functions and organs are less resistant. The natural elimination process of toxins and wastes is also undermined. The ability of the body and organs to benefit from essential food ingredients such as vitamins, minerals, and oligo-elements is reduced. Overall resistance to various kinds of physical aggressions is also diminished. Such deficiencies add-up and may lead to the end of earthly life.

The average life expectancy being between 80 and 85 years, it confirms that most humans are fragilized when they reach that age bracket, often to the point of no-return. This is enhanced by the return of Uranus on its original position, as seen in chapter 5.

There are exceptions of course. More and more people live to be a hundred and more. Protecting configurations in their birth chart are certainly indicative of such exceptional potential. They are useful to withstand the pressures during the difficult transits period of their life.

My partner's grandmother, Umeko Fukui, is one of them. She was born in Osaka on the last day in 1910 and is still alive today (February 2021). She is 110 years old and well cared for. She has only recently lost most of her memory, but she is physiologically quite fit! Can you see in her chart what configurations indicate her extraordinary resistance to the effect of time? In her chart, Pluto is in Gemini, sextile Saturn, and trine Chiron which is sextile Saturn. This beneficial triangle has helped her a lot in many ways. Saturn is "her planet" because it rules her sun sign, Capricorn. It forms a sextile with Pluto that amplifies the regenerating potential and the life potential. There are five "planets" in Capricorn: The Sun, the

Moon, Mercury, Venus, and Uranus. They are all represented by Saturn. Jupiter plays a positive role too through a sextile with the Moon. And it is in Pluto's sign.

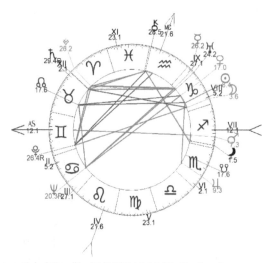

Fukui Umeko 31/12/1910 15:00 Osaka, Japan

☉	♄	♂	♃	♀	☿	♄	
☽	♄	♂	♃	♀	☿	♄	
☿	♄	♂	♃	♀	☿	♄	
♀	♄	♂	♃	♀	☿	♄	
♂	♃	♀	☿	♄	♂	♃	
⛢	♂	♃	♀	☿	♄	♂	
♃	♀	☿	♄	♂	♃	♀	
♄	♂	♃	♀	☿	♄	♂	
⚷	♆	♄	♂	♃	♀	☿	♄
⛢	♄	♂	♃	♀	☿	♄	
♆	☽	♄	♂	♃	♀	☿	♄
♀	☿	♄	♂	♃	♀	☿	

The dominant in Umeko's chart is Saturn, with a score of seven ends of chains. It is in Aries, a sign showing strength and combativity. There is no doubt that Saturn and Mars have helped this person to. It gave this person the will to survive and impose herself as a business owner and head of family after the untimely loss of her parents. The time factor represented by Saturn is definitely on her side. ☺

In the chart, the elements in Capricorn are under pressure due to discordant aspects with Saturn and Neptune. Umeko's life has not been an easy one indeed, but here resilience and regenerating capacity protected her from the worst and allowed here to still be alive more than a hundred and ten years after her birth.

Pluto is in Gemini, a sign ruled by Mercury found in Capricorn, not far from Uranus, Venus, the Sun, and the Moon, all in Saturn's sign. Difficulties, obstacles, and hardship are represented by Saturn. The discordant configurations amplify the role of Saturn. They say that "what does not kill you makes you stronger". In Umeko's case, this is 100% true. Note also that Mercury is the ruler of the Ascendant in Gemini. Its position in Capricorn reinforces the potential of this sign and, by extension, the potential of Saturn, while the Ascendant in Gemini allowed a more flexible and adaptable nature to deal more efficiently and "lightly" with difficulties in unfortunate circumstances.

We can add to this short reading the trine aspect linking Chiron with Pluto. Chiron is in Aquarius, as sign rules by Uranus, found in Capricorn, once more reinforcing the role of Saturn. This aspect has also been extremely useful to retain an optimum state of health with no major illnesses to deplore, except for hip surgery to replace worn articulation (Capricorn) when Umeko was in her early eighties.

The sextiles formed by Jupiter with the Sun and the Moon are two other major assets to preserve a more positive approach in presence of difficulties to solve many problems and benefit from a certain amount of luck and providential opportunities. These aspects are also act on blood pressure to keep it at the right level.

See what Pluto may produce in your life when it opposes itself and other elements in your chart. Use the list of aphorisms in the following pages to guide your reading. Bear in mind that they are only a glimpse of what you can expect from the various configurations formed by transiting Pluto with the rest of your chart.

The transiting aspects of Pluto

Pluto in harmony with the Sun

During this long period, the vital energy and drive are greatly supported by the regenerating influence of Pluto. Its positive influence is also appreciated health wise. Great transformations are made possible with determination and endurance, particularly observed in the areas represented by the Houses in Leo (Sun) and Scorpio (Pluto) and the House where Pluto transits.

Pluto in dissonance with the Sun

This transit is likely to produce diverse problems with profound consequences more likely to occur in the areas represented by the Sun and Pluto in the chart. It has a detrimental effect on vitality and general health. It creates a darker approach to what life imposes. The conjunction is forcing a blend of life (Sun) and death (Pluto) from which is seems quite difficult to obtain a positive combination. The areas represented by the Houses in Leo (Sun) and Scorpio (Pluto) and where Pluto is transiting are also concerned.

Pluto in harmony with the Moon

The positive influence of Pluto helps deal with the more intimate aspects of life. It increases emotional resilience and allows more efficiency from sustained efforts to deal with difficulties. It is also useful to preserve or restore health, as the Moon plays a major role on body fluids and glandular activity. The areas represented by the Houses in Cancer (Moon) and Scorpio (Pluto) and the House where Pluto transits are also favoured.

Pluto in dissonance with the Moon

A feeling of increased sensibility is likely to make life less enjoyable and produce a more pessimistic emotional mindset. Family and close surroundings may be marked by profound transformation and unfortunate circumstances and events. Health may also suffer from the influence of Pluto because of increased vulnerability to contaminations or disturbed glandular function. The areas represented by the Houses in Cancer (Moon) and Scorpio (Pluto) and the House where Pluto transits are also concerned.

Pluto in harmony with Mercury

This transit is a source of cerebral strength and increased depth of thought that is useful to solve intricate problems with patience and endurance. Favourable to students, it enhances the power of concentration and observation. Memory and difficult mental efforts are favoured. The areas represented by the Houses in Gemini (Mercury) and Scorpio (Pluto) and the House where Pluto transits are primarily concerned.

Pluto in dissonance with Mercury

During this long period, the intellect is subject to a profound mutation. Dark ideas and negative thinking make it difficult to cheerfully deal with personal dans social relationships. Self-image is deteriorated and becomes a source of intellectual negation of life in general. The areas represented by the Houses in Gemini (Mercury) and Scorpio (Pluto) and the House where Pluto transits are also concerned.

Pluto in harmony with Venus

During this transit, creation and procreation potentials are enhanced. There is a deeper approach to love, romance, art, and food (Venus: the good things of life). Pluto also helps heal from various health disorders and intimate setbacks. The ability to withstand hardship positively favours profound transformation and major realisations in the areas represented by both planets in the chart (Houses in Taurus and Scorpio) and by the House where Pluto is transiting.

Pluto in dissonance with Venus

This period is likely to be marked by intimate difficulties, romantic setbacks and dissatisfaction issued from a tendency to behave in a more distractive than constructive manner. Profound suffering may be viewed as a proof of being alive. Artists are often at their best when painful circumstances make them feel deeply sorry for themselves. The areas represented by the Houses in Taurus (Venus) and Scorpio (Pluto) and the House where Pluto is transiting are also concerned.

Pluto in harmony with Mars

The combined energies of both planets are a great asset during this transit. Pluto not only amplifies the active potential represented by Mars, but it also makes it more resilient and profound. The results obtained have a unique positive and long-lasting connotation. Health and the ability to surmount major obstacles are also indicated. The areas represented by the Houses in Aries (Mars) and Scorpio (Pluto) and where Pluto is transiting are also concerned.

Pluto in dissonance with Mars

This is a long period during which the active potential tends to turn around to become a source of major setbacks and forced transformations. Radicality is amplified, accentuating the risks of conflicts, incidents, and accidents. Sudden health concerns are likely to increase the degree of general dissatisfaction. The areas represented by the Houses in Aries (Mars) and Scorpio (Pluto) and where Pluto is transiting are also concerned.

Pluto in harmony with Vesta

Balance and harmony being major factors of wellbeing, during this long transit of Pluto, the potential to preserve or restore such positive position is greatly amplified and favoured. The ability to sustain long-lasting effort and obtain the best results is another asset derived from this beneficial transit of Pluto. The areas represented by the Houses in Libra (Vesta) and Scorpio (Pluto) and where Pluto is transiting are also concerned.

Pluto in dissonance with Vesta

During this transit, the foundations, and the meaning of life in accordance with the notions of balance and harmony are deeply questioned and undergo complete transformation. There may be a tendency to feel victim of unfortunate circumstances which enhances inner instability and self-questioning. The areas represented by the Houses in Libra (Vesta) and Scorpio (Pluto) and where Pluto is transiting are also concerned.

Pluto in harmony with Jupiter

This transit enhances the potential to succeed, thanks to more determination and strength to overcome obstacles while benefiting from major opportunities. Health is protected by the regenerating influence of Pluto. A more positive and philosophic appreciation of life makes it easier to deal with problems and find positive solutions. The areas represented by the Houses in Sagittarius (Jupiter) and Scorpio (Pluto) and where Pluto is transiting are also concerned.

Pluto in dissonance with Jupiter

What has been overlooked or neglected during the preceding harmonious transit of Pluto becomes a source of gloomy questioning. The notion of "destruction in view of reconstruction" applies and may affect life in various ways. Health is subject to long periods of indisposition that may need major treatments. The areas represented by the Houses in Sagittarius (Jupiter) and Scorpio (Pluto) and where Pluto is transiting are also concerned.

Pluto in harmony with Saturn

Patience and determination are essential qualities to climb to the summit and succeed durably. Pluto and Saturn offer accrued resistance to pain, effort, and difficulties. Time becomes a major asset that allows much to be done outside the usual parameters and limitations. These potentials are a source of solid health protection. The areas represented by the Houses in Capricorn (Saturn) and Scorpio (Pluto) and where Pluto is transiting are also concerned.

Pluto in dissonance with Saturn

During this transit, time is likely to become a source of concern. It may be due to old age, but it is also linked to the notion of destruction of what has been built or acquired. Karma plays a dominant role to explain the degree of difficulties to address and deal with. General state of health is disturbed by the influence of Pluto. Bones or joints may become painful due to loss of calcium and essential minerals. The areas represented by the Houses in Capricorn (Saturn) and Scorpio (Pluto) and where Pluto is transiting are also concerned.

Pluto in harmony with Chiron

This type of transit is a profound source of protection and resistance to occasional health disorders. It has a positive influence on the ability to think rationally and to find concrete solutions to many problems. Intricate and precision tasks are more easily taken care of. The areas represented by the Houses in Virgo (Chiron) and Scorpio (Pluto) and where Pluto is transiting are also concerned.

Pluto in dissonance with Chiron

During this transit it is of upmost important to take care not to do anything that would threaten the general state of health. The ability to observe and analyse rationally is less efficient and tinted by darker thoughts and presumptions. An effort is necessary to keep in good shape, but it is usually mot enough to prevent disorders. The areas represented by the Houses in Virgo (Chiron) and Scorpio (Pluto) and where Pluto is transiting are also concerned.

Pluto in harmony with Uranus

Major changes with profound and durable consequences are likely to improve life in many unexpected manners. Odd circumstances and opportunities become a source of complete transformation. Inventiveness and originality are in tune with the deeper reality of life and death, making it possible to find regeneration in unexplored areas with much success and satisfaction. The areas represented by the Houses in Aquarius (Uranus) and Scorpio (Pluto) and where Pluto is transiting are also concerned.

Pluto in dissonance with Uranus

Unexpected drastic changes are likely during this type of transit. They have a profound regenerating influence and impose the need to accept to lose to derive more positive results from unfortunate experiences and their destructive connotation. Health condition may deteriorate suddenly and durably. The areas represented by the Houses in Aquarius (Uranus) and Scorpio (Pluto) and where Pluto is transiting are also concerned.

Pluto in harmony with Neptune

This type of transit puts the emphasis on the spiritual connexion with the notions of life and death. A lofty approach to important earthly matters helps make problems easier to understand, accept and solution. Health also benefits from the regenerating energy of Pluto, with durable consequences. The areas represented by the Houses in Pisces (Neptune) and Scorpio (Pluto) and where Pluto is transiting are also concerned.

Pluto in dissonance with Neptune

Faith is not enough during this type of transit to compensate the loss of trust in earthly life and self-confidence. Spiritual and karmic experiences are likely to produce profound questioning and a need for answer of a loftier nature. Health disorders are mainly due to hormonal imbalance and a to a darker or negative approach to medical treatments. The areas represented by the Houses in Pisces (Neptune) and Scorpio (Pluto) and where Pluto is transiting are also concerned.

Pluto in harmony with Pluto

This type of transit (sextile and trine) reinforces the regenerating potential of both body and mind. It produces more positive energy to combat, surmount or deals with life's difficulties. More tenacity and determination favour durable success. Much can be done during such a long period of positive influence. Besides the obvious physiological and psychological protection, this transit also favours the areas represented by Pluto (House in Scorpio) the House where it is found in the chart and where it is transiting.

Pluto in dissonance with Pluto

During this period, the regeneration potential is significantly lowered. Pluto acts on itself like a source of pollution, both physiological and psychological. Darkness seems to attract and motivate negative thinking and even self-destructive tendencies. Health may be deeply affected by contamination or poisoning. This can symbolically be expressed in the areas ruled by Pluto (House in

Scorpio), by the House where it is found in the chart, and where it is transiting.

Pluto in harmony with the Ascendant
This transit intensifies the role of the inner self to improve authenticity and the ability to impose oneself according to the more subtle facets of personality. Determination and endurance enhance the potential to succeed durably. Such positive energy often comes from the areas of life represented by the House where Pluto is transiting and where it imposes profound transformations. The House in Scorpio is also concerned and should be analysed to determine its role in the evolution bestowed by Pluto.

Pluto in dissonance with the Ascendant

During this long period, the self is confronted to major questioning and inner turmoil. There is a nihilistic tendency to the detriment of the "joie de vivre" and general wellbeing. Self-confidence is under pressure due to unfortunate circumstances that remind of the vulnerability of human life. The areas represented by the House in Scorpio are concerned, while the difficulties are likely to come from those represented by the House where Pluto is transiting.

Pluto in harmony with the Mid-Heaven
During this long period, tenacity and resilience characterise the way projects are taken car of. The potential to succeed is reinforced, while goals and responsibilities are renewed sources of strong motivation. Pluto's energy also favours family life and relationships with close-ones. The areas represented by the House in Scorpio may be the origin of the increase in enthusiasm and determination, together with those represented by the House where Pluto is transiting.

Pluto in dissonance with the Mid-Heaven
This type of transits makes it difficult to keep on climbing the social ladder or to fulfil important social or professional responsibilities. Unfortunate events may play a detrimental role with major long-lasting consequences. A negative approach to career and work may

stem from familial or conjugal difficulties. The problems to solve may come from the areas represented by the House in Scorpio and the House where Pluto is transiting.

* * * * * * * * * *

Once again, bear in mind that the above interpretations are just a guide. They should not be taken for a finish product to copy-paste to fill any astrological forecasts. Also, remember that while Pluto transits somewhere around the zodiac, other important transits occur. They may support or distort and temper Pluto's influence. You need to synthesise the data to make your reading precise and useful.

Lesson 8

THE TRANSITS IN THE HOUSES

In this lesson, we are going to deal with the influence of the transits when the object concerned forms a conjunction with the cusp of a House with repercussions while the transit lasts. According to the aspects formed with other objects and elements in the chart, such transits can produce memorable events of all kinds in the areas represented by the Houses concerned.

As a backdrop of the period marked by the transit in a House, a basic analysis of that House in relation with the rest of the chart is necessary to obtain a more personal reading of the transit in question.

The contact with the cusp of a House triggers the influence of the element (planet, luminary[13], asteroid, nodes, etc.). The effect then propagates through the House and the areas of life it represents, in relation with the areas represented by the House ruled by the transiting element.

The precise moment when a conjunction with the cusp of a House occurs depends on the exactness of the time of birth which determined the positions of the twelve Houses around the chart. Note that there are numerous systems to "domify" a chart. I use the Placidus system. In the US, the equal-house system is often preferred. You are free to chose according to your preference or astrological knowledge background.

The cusp of a House progresses by about one degree around the chart every four minutes or earthly time. We know that the time of birth is rarely recorded precisely. Hence, many birth charts are wrong. Even if it is only by five or ten minutes, the cusps of the Houses change places, and in some cases, they also change signs.

The date of entry of a fast planet is not affected by very much more than a few days, but the slow planets, such as Uranus, Neptune and

---

[13] The "luminaries" are the Sun and the Moon.

Pluto, their transit in a House would be modified by a few months to a few years!

In the example chart number 1 below, the time of birth is 10 minutes less than in the example chart number 2.

Example chart 1

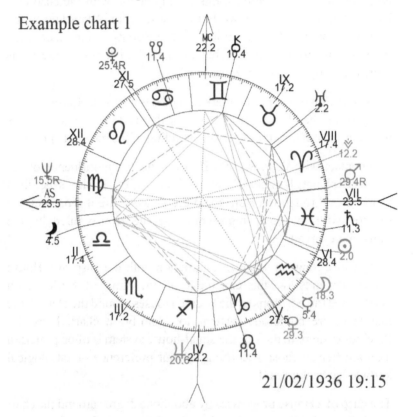

21/02/1936 19:15

In example 1, the cusps of Houses VI and XII are in Aquarius and Leo. In the chart on the right, they are in Pisces and Virgo.

The Ascendant begins at 23.5° in Virgo in example 1, and at 25.4° in the example 2. The difference is small (under 2°) but significant when it comes to the transits of the three slower planets: Uranus, Neptune, and Pluto.

Example chart 2

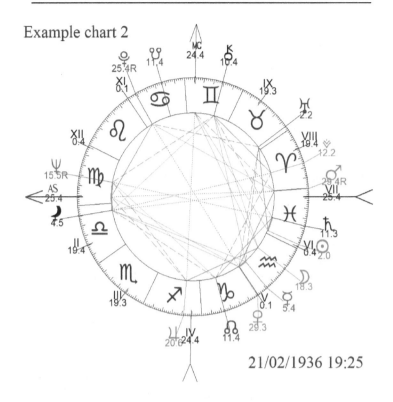

21/02/1936 19:25

Uranus takes 7 years to transit a sign. A difference of 2° corresponds to almost 6 months. Neptune takes 14 years to transit a sign. A difference of 2° corresponds to more than 11 months. Knowing that Pluto can take one to two years to progress by only 1° around the chart, a difference of 2° would correspond to two to four years!

Have your time of birth verified and rectified by a competent astrologer for the dates of the transits of the slow planets to be right. A precise time of birth leads to a precise chart and to more precise astrological forecasts.

But what is the time of birth?

Is it the moment the child is entirely out of the mother's womb? Is it the moment they cut the umbilical cord? Some astrologers estimate that it is the moment the head alone is entirely out. My opinion is that it should be when the child is entirely out, although there are only a few minutes between the moment when the head is out followed by the whole body.

What about the caesarean? I am occasionally told "I was born by caesarean. Does it count?" Of course, it counts. Besides this kind of birth always shows in a birth chart. The cusp of the Ascendant is usually involved in revealing configurations.

Determining your exact time of birth (TOB)

As explained earlier, it is possible and often necessary to verify and rectify the time of birth. This done using various techniques. I do this quite often for people who are unsure of their exact time of birth. If you need to ask for this service, visit the school's website where you will find the relevant information, or ask a competent astrologer.

My practice of forecasting with astrology has progressively demonstrated that the influence of a transit in a House begins as soon as the planet concerned enters the sign where the House's cusp is. The ensuing period until the conjunction with the cusp of the House is comparable to a "gestation" phase during which it is advised to prepare for the entry of the planet in the House.

When a slow planet in transit approaches the cusp of a House, its energy stimulates the areas of life represented by that House. Meanwhile, if a faster planet passes by to form a conjunction with the slower one, can have a triggering effect of the influence of the slower planet with significant repercussions in the areas concerned.

For example, in a birth chart, transiting Uranus is about to form a conjunction with the cusp of the fifth House. It is difficult to determine the precise date of such a slow transit.

The entry of Uranus in a House is a unique event because this planet takes 84 years to do a complete revolution of the zodiac. The events occurring during such transit often create irreversible changes in the areas represented by the House concerned.

In our example, drastic changes are expected in the sectors of life linked to House V. These changes can be very different from one person to another. Uranus can indicate: the conception of a child, a major artistic opportunity, the birth of a unique sentimental relationship, an extraordinary strike of like, or any other unexpected most important event in relation with House V.

To determine a precise date, the faster transits are used. The Sun, Mercury, Venus, or Mars can play the triggering role. Here is what happened to a person I did a reading for some years ago.

I will call this client John. In John's chart, House V begins at 8°41' in a sign. For a long time prior to the consultation, John's sentimental life was not a problem. He had no particular question about this area during our meeting. A well-established marriage and a family seemed to fulfill his needs and allow him to put his mind to his professional activity quite successfully. While reading his chart, however, I noticed that Uranus was about to enter the fifth House. Looking into the ephemerides, I was able to determine the precise date of the event. I explained to John that the influence of Uranus could radically change his sentimental life. Then I noticed that Venus was approaching to form an exact conjunction with Uranus precisely on the cusp of House V, where was transiting too. I assumed that Venus and Mars could indicate "love at first sight", but I kept on investigating the situation which led me to the Moon's position. Coincidence or not, I notice that on the day of the consultation, the Moon is transiting John's Ascendant and conjunct the North Lunar Node. I explained to John that his life was probably about to take a drastic turn produced by an unexpected opportunity or from an extraordinary encounter with someone exceptional.

John was not convinced at all and we therefore concentrated on a reading about his professional activity and projects.

A short time later, John asked for an urgent consultation and provided the birth data of a young woman he met a few days after our initial meeting. The event seemed to have completely changed his life. Examining the woman's birth chart, I noticed that Uranus formed a transiting conjunction with the cusp of her fourth House (family and residence). The same transits of Venus and Mars accompanied Uranus in a similar manner to what is explained earlier. John said that he had never felt such a strong attraction in his life ever before. He said his new friend (lover) felt the same about him. Comparing both charts left no doubt about the strength and long-lasting potential of this all new relationship.

This story illustrates the importance of certain transits. Uranus is the only planet to complete a revolution of the zodiac during a human lifetime. Its capacity to produce radical changes is exceptional. When faster transits back the influence of Uranus, its natural potential is multiplied tenfold. The areas represented by the Houses involved are primarily concerned.

Here is an example to illustrate this theory.

In a birth chart, Jupiter is transiting House II. It slowly approaches to form a conjunction with the natal position of Venus in this House. To analyse the possible effect of this transit, we must take note of the usual influence of Jupiter in House II. It is linked to the idea of financial evolution and success.

In this chart (reproduced on the next page), House II is in Taurus. Venus is therefore the ruler of this House. It is also the "natural" ruler of House II, symbolically linked to Taurus. Venus would therefore have a beneficial influence that could prove very useful on a material or financial point of view. The luck factor is not negligeable and would favour success in the person's life.

The effect of transiting Jupiter is to boost the latent energy of Venus and its positive potential. While it lasts, many opportunities are likely to produce very good results. The main source of revenues (work or other source) is greatly improved by the powerful Jovian influence. This transit is rare enough to be seriously taken into consideration, but its influence differs every twelve years. It is never exactly the same because Jupiter is also submitted to the influences of other planets in transit around the zodiac during the same period.

There was a time when I applied the common rule about "beneficial" and "detrimental" planets. Years of practice demonstrated that all planets had a double and even triple type of energy: harmonic, dissonant, and neutral.

The influence of a planets depends on its natal position, on the type of transit, on the aspects formed within the birth chart and during the transit. A dominant planet in a birth chart would be less a problem during dissonant transiting aspects. However, this is not an infallible rule. Mars in Aries, for example, is strong in its sign of rulership. This does not ensure that it will not be a source of tension, incidents, or accidents, during its dissonant transits. On the contrary, it seems that the god of war is more virulent and a source of mishaps during a dissonant transit if it is in its sign of rulership in the birth chart. It is also more beneficial when the transit is harmonious.

Lesson 9

THE SLOW TRANSITS IN THE HOUSES

The first of the slow planets is Jupiter. It takes Jupiter around one year to transit one complete sign. But it can remain much longer in a House depending on its size.

However, the influence of a planet in a House begins as soon as it enters the sign in which that House begin, even though it may be near the end of the sign.

To help you understand this concept, imagine that you are in a swimming pool. You could be close to the diving board, half-way through the pool, or near the far end of that pool. Suddenly, you notice John, a friend, dive, and swim toward you. From the moment John is the water, you can feel his energy and his influence on you. It becomes stronger and stronger until he reaches you wherever you are in the pool. If you appreciate John, you rejoice at the idea of enjoying a moment in the pool with him. If you do not really appreciate John, you know you still have to greet him, and to spend some time forcing yourself to be cheerful. In both cases, you have a bit of time to prepare for the encounter, but John's incidence on the quality of the moment begins as soon as you see him dive to join you.

When a planet enters a sign, its energy acts as a signal to the House positioned in that sign. It produces "wave forms" that quickly reach the House concerned and the areas of life it represents. The time the planets takes to reach the cusp of the House in question must be used to prepare for the encounter and its possible effect.

In my client's case, the entry of Uranus in the sign dated back more than two years before it became really active through the conjunction it formed with the cusp of the fifth House in his chart. That period had been sentimentally ambiguous and uncomfortable. The man was unconsciously in search of romantic improvement. The lady he met, was also in an uneasy situation. Her marriage was failing and disappointing. Their life concretely changed when Uranus reached the cusp of House V in the man's chart, and House IV in the woman's chart.

Let us begin the study of the transits of the planets in the Houses, by the slowest one, Pluto.

PLUTO

The exact moment of a transiting conjunction between Pluto and the cusp of a House is difficult to determine precisely. Firstly because of the extremely slow speed of this planet, and secondly because the time of birth is rarely exact, as explained earlier in this book. In one year, Pluto only progresses by 1° or 2° in a sign. Pluto's speed of revolution depends on the region of the zodiac it is transiting. As seen earlier, due to its eccentric orbit, Pluto can remain more than thirty years in certain signs and less than twelve years in others.

For example, on 1st January 1918, Pluto was standing at 4°23' in Cancer.

On 31st December of that same year, il had only moved to 5°53' in the same sign. This is a progression of just 1°10' in one year! By comparison, the Moon merely needs two hours to cover such a short distance around the zodiac.

On 1st January 2004, Pluto was standing at 20°30' in Sagittarius.

On 31st December of that same year, it was found at 22°41' in Sagittarius, a considerable evolution of 2°11'compared to 1°104 in 1918. Pluto remained twelve years in Sagittarius and more than thirty years in Cancer.

The role of Pluto is to regenerate the areas of life represented by the House where it is transiting. Regeneration also means transformation. Pluto acts as a "cleaner" (occasionally as an undertaker…) because regeneration implies that "something must die or be destroyed to be born again on new or different grounds.

For example, when Pluto transits the cusp of the Ascendant, it announces a long period of inner transformation with profound repercussions in intimate relationships and private life. The self is confronted to the need for total restoration. Pluto imposes deep cleaning to bring forward inner truth and authenticity.

Long before it reaches the cusp of the Ascendant (House I) Pluto transits in House XII corresponding to the notion of gestation and preparation. Thus, what happens when Pluto arrives in the Ascendant, is not unexpected. On the contrary, what happens then entirely depends on the degree of implication in the project of somehow being "born again".

According to age, health, and social or professional situation, the transit of Pluto in the Ascendant can be quite destructive. However, such "destruction" is part of the rebirth process. There is a strong karmic meaning and resonance to this transit. As expressed earlier, with Pluto, "what does not kill you makes you stronger". In fact, what really kills us makes us stronger on the spiritual point of view according to the cycles of incarnations necessary to progress spiritually. Not everyone lives through a transit of Pluto in the Ascendant. This is due to its slow revolution speed around the zodiac. If your Ascendant is in Taurus for example, you will have to wait until 2098-99 to see a transit of Pluto happen. As seen earlier in this book, Pluto takes 248 years to complete its journey around the zodiac.

In the following pages, you will find a list of aphorisms to help you interpret the possible effects of the transits of Pluto in each one of the twelve Houses. Please, remember that those texts are just meant as a guide, and that a planet in transit never acts alone. Other planets intervene to enhance or limit the influence of Pluto. Take every aspect of the chart in consideration before delivering a forecast.

THE TRANSITS OF PLUTO IN THE HOUSES

The influence of Pluto can last many years while it transits through a House. It is more remarkable around the time when it enters or is close to the cusp of the House. Later, faster transits in conjunction with Pluto occasionally trigger its basic energy and role in the areas represented by the House concerned.

* * * * * * * * * *

House I (Ascendant)
This transit announces a profound regeneration where the notions of dying and being born again prevail and are a source of deep questioning about the mystery of life and death. Close relationships are put to the test in a karmic way. The areas represented by the House in Scorpio are linked to the overall tendency of this period.

House II
This transit is likely to produce a complete regeneration of the material value of life. Finances are subject to profound questioning due to important losses and a nihilistic tendency when it comes to money and earthly possessions. The areas represented by the House in Scorpio are linked to the transformations occurring in this House.

House III
During this long period, Pluto produces a profound need for mental regeneration. Life is perceived differently due to unpleasant or painful circumstances involving siblings. A deeper interest in the mysteries of life and death is indicated. The areas represented by the House in Scorpio are linked to the intellectual transformation occurring in this House.

House IV
This transit is known to produce major transformation in the family and place of residence. The notions of destruction in view of reconstruction apply to the close environment, both human and geographical. The areas represented by the House in Scorpio are linked to the transformation process occurring in this House.

House V

During this transit, unfortunate circumstances are likely to impose a profound transformation of the perception of love, romance, children, and/or artistic creativity. The areas represented by the House in Scorpio are linked to the transformation process produced by the regenerative influence of Pluto.

House VI

This transit is likely to produce a profound and uncontrollable need to transform the work environment radically and deeply with important professional consequences. Health may play a major role in the decision taken. The areas represented by the House in Scorpio are linked to the transformation process produced by the regenerative influence of Pluto.

House VII

This transit corresponds to a profound need to question the value of close relationships such as marriage and other important personal, social, and professional partnerships. Regeneration in this area may be imposed by unfortunate events of karmic connotation. The areas represented by the House in Scorpio are linked to the transformation process produced by Pluto.

House VIII

Pluto being the "natural ruler" of this House, its transiting influence in House VIII is strong. It emphasises the notion of destruction and reconstruction (to die and be born again). It imposes a complete revision of material values. It increases the interest and questioning about the mysteries of life. The areas represented by the House in Scorpio play a dominant role during this transit of Pluto.

House IX

During this transit, profound changes are likely to have a determining influence on the philosophical approach to life and death. The need to radically transform the social order by questioning the real value of laws and regulations may produce adverse behaviour with unfortunate consequences. The areas represented by the House in Scorpio play a dominant role during this transit of Pluto.

House X (MC)

A complete transformation of social status, career and major projects is likely. There may be crucial repercussions in family life and situation by opposition to House IV. Unfortunate circumstances are often responsible for total reviewing of the importance of success and social status. The areas represented by the House in Scorpio play a dominant role during this transit of Pluto.

House XI

Both human and geographical environments are subject to a complete transformation process often due to unfortunate events and their detrimental impact on the value of friendship and social interaction. Others are a source of obscure thoughts that trigger adverse reactions. The areas represented by the House in Scorpio play a dominant role during this transit of Pluto.

House XII

This transit has a deep karmic connotation. It imposes a profound transformation of spiritual values with definitive consequences. The notion of gestation linked to an important project or situation may lead to a new birth potential when Pluto reaches the cusp of the Ascendant some years later. The areas represented by the House in Scorpio play a dominant role during this crucial transit of Pluto.

Lesson 10

NEPTUNE

The transits of Neptune are a little faster than Pluto's, but twice as slow as those of Uranus. Neptune takes 165 years to turn around the zodiac. Its influence is said to create confusion and uncertainty, together with irrationality and haziness. Neptune envelopes or dispenses a sort of vapour or cloudy atmosphere in the areas represented by the House transited. It slows down the process of rigorous analysis with detrimental effect on the ability to deal with the reality of life appropriately.

However, beliefs and imagination, intuition and inspiration occasionally take the lead and produce extraordinary effects and great results. The spiritual dimension enhances the potential to obtain subtle information that feeds personal motivation to realise the dream or the ideal it is meant for. The connexion becomes an efficient means to take a higher point of view and get a global vision on life that allows easier detection of flaws and imperfections. In that sense, Neptune's influence is extremely positive and helpful.

Knowing that Neptune takes fourteen years to transit one full sign and that a House can be much larger, the nebulosity this planet produces can last a long time. It is therefore necessary to turn to other faster transits and combine their influences with Neptune's to better understand, appreciate and integrate its role in the astrological forecast.

As with Pluto, it is difficult to precisely date the entry of Neptune in a House if not completely sure of the time of birth. Because it only moves by two to three degrees a year, a variation of five or ten minutes of the birth time is equivalent to more than twelve months difference in Neptune's moment of entry in the House concerned. In fact, like all other transits, Neptune affects the areas of life represented by a House as soon as it enters the sign where the House begins.

Next is a list of short aphorisms to help you understand the role of Neptune in transit in each one of the twelve Houses. Once again, do not rely on my prose to finalise your forecasts.

Rely on your own words and ability to blend planetary transits rather than analyse them individually.

THE TRANSITS OF NEPTUNE IN THE HOUSES

The influence of transiting Neptune can last for many years in a House. It is more remarkable around the time when it enters or is close to the cusp of the House. Meanwhile, faster transits in conjunction with Neptune occasionally trigger its basic energy and role in the areas represented by the House concerned.

* * * * * * * * * *

House I (Ascendant)

This transit increases the natural connexion with the spiritual reality of life. However, it can also increase inner confusion and uncertainty. Extraordinary experiences as well as illness may produce bewilderment and loss of concrete purpose. The areas represented by the House in Pisces contribute to the influence of Neptune during such a long journey in the Ascendant.

House II

Neptune here can either favour or prevent financial success. Confused feeding habits and allergic reactions are also indicated. Intuition may be quite propitious in business ventures, but it can also lead to errors due to a tendency to act on belief rather than on verified data. The areas represented by the House in Pisces contribute to the role of transiting Neptune.

House III

During this transit, the intellect relies more on intuitive thinking than rational observation. It can be useful to communicate spontaneously. Neptune enhances inspiration and spiritual creativity. It can also create mental confusion and uncertainty. The areas represented by the House in Pisces contributes to the influence of transiting Neptune.

House IV

This transit is likely to have a troubling influence on family affairs and human and geographical environments. Strange events and situations become a factor of confusion and uncertainty. The quest for the ideal place can be a source of inner questioning and passive motivation. The areas represented by the House in Pisces contribute to the influence of this transit of Neptune.

House V

This transit is likely to increase creativity and the need for love and romance. Intuition may increase luck and become a source of success and enrichment. However, Neptune can produce more confusion and uncertainty than satisfying concrete results. The areas represented by the House in Pisces contribute to the influence of this transit.

House VI

This period is likely to be marked by a tendency to hope and believe more than to act rationally to obtain the best results in daily duties. Uncertainty at work is indicated. Neptune may produce troubling physiological reactions such as allergies or psychosomatic disorders. The areas represented by the House in Pisces contribute to the influence of this transit of Neptune.

House VII

During this transit, uncertainty, and confusion colour important relationships. The influence of others on personal decisions is likely to increase the risk of errors and disappointment. But Neptune can also announce the realisation of an extraordinary partnership. The areas represented by the House in Pisces contribute to the influence of this transit of Neptune.

House VIII

Finances may be a source of confusion and uncertainty due to Neptune's influence on the rational approach needed to handle money matters adequately. Death and the mysteries of life contribute to inner questioning and doubt, while potentially improving finances in an extraordinary manner. The areas represented by the House in Pisces contribute to the influence of this transit of Neptune.

House IX

Social matters, rules, regulations, and laws are likely to become a source of confusion and uncertainty. An idealistic approach to knowledge contributes to involvements in unusual courses and studies to improve the quality of life in a lofty and philosophical way. The areas represented by the House in Pisces contribute to the influence of this transit of Neptune.

House X (MC)
Uncertainty and confusion are likely to become sources of errors to the detriment of social and/or professional status. Neptune can also announce very unusual situations, events, or opportunities with extraordinary implications at the highest level. The areas represented by the House in Pisces contribute to the influence of this transit of Neptune.

House XI
The human and geographical environment becomes confused and uncertain during this transit. Encounters with extraordinary individuals are likely to have a spiritual or karmic connotation and meaning. Lofty relationships can develop into highly valuable partnerships or disastrous disillusions. The areas represented by the House in Pisces contribute to the influence of this transit of Neptune.

House XII
Here, Neptune is in natural rulership which makes its influence stronger and more meaningful. It can greatly increase confusion, both physical (illness) or mental (inner questioning on a spiritual level). Intuition and soul sensibility are greatly increased. Astral travel and extraordinary oneiric activity are often a result of the influence of Neptune here. The areas represented by the House in Pisces contribute to the influence of this transit.

Lesson 11

URANUS

The entry of Uranus in a House signals the imminence of radical and irreversible changes in the areas represented by the House concerned. Uranus takes 84 years to complete a revolution around the zodiac. It therefore transits a House only once in a lifetime. The conjunction with the cusp of a House is a unique phenomenon, except for those who live well over the ripe age of 84. Uranus produces unexpected and exceptional changes.

You cannot imagine what Uranus is able to do and how it is going to happen. However, for some of us, the transits of this planet may not engender any significant transformation. The reason is that the strength of Uranus depends on its position and importance in their birth chart. Rest assured that for most of us, the arrival of this planet coincides with unprecedented modifications of their life in the most extraordinary manner.

Such changes can be either beneficial or malevolent, according to various configurations involving Uranus in the birth chart and at the time of the transit. You will need to consider these points before delivering any significant prognostic or forecast.

Uranus remains around seven years in each sign, including periods of retrogradation when its energy goes into a sort of standby position. It may also be considered as a "gestation" period, useful to get ready or to prepare for the renewed influence of the planet when it resumes its direct motion. Consult the ephemerides to take note of the periods of retrogradation which can last five to six months.

Depending on the size of a House, unless you use the equal-house system, a transit of Uranus can last from three or four, to more than fourteen years. As you know, the dispositions of the Houses depend on the latitude of birth. They are equal around the equator, but quite different the farther north or south the place of birth is.

A birth chart established for Paris, France, in spring is different to a winter chart for the same location. With an Ascendant in the same sign, both charts show considerable variations in the dispositions of the Houses around the charts. See the examples below to illustrate this fact.

Springtime birth

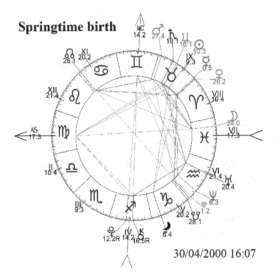

30/04/2000 16:07

Winter time birth

15/01/2001 16:07

In the first chart established for the 30th of April, each House belongs to one sign. In the second chart established for the 15th of January, House V begins in Libra and includes Scorpio, the following sign entirely, and House VI begins in Sagittarius. House XI also includes the following sign. Those following signs are said to be "intercepted". Note how the positions of the MC (Mid Heaven) differ from one chart to the other.

When day-time is almost equal to night-time, the Houses are almost equal. When day-time or night-time is longer, the cusps of the Houses are disposed more unevenly as spring moves toward summer or autumn toward winter.

That is why a transit through a House can last much longer than through a sign. It can also be much shorter when, for example, two Houses begin in the same sign. See the second chart where Houses I and II begin in Cancer; and Houses VII and VIII in Capricorn. Houses I and VII are only 17° wide. In that case, a transit of Uranus lasts for three and a half to four years instead of seven years to transit through a full sign of 30°…

In the first example chart, Uranus remains approximately seven years in Houses V and XI. In the second chart, it needs almost ten years to transit each of those Houses.

During its journey through a House, Uranus produces profound changes with definitive repercussions and modifications in the areas represented by the House concerned. Freedom and independence are represented by Uranus. Its transits confer a stronger than ever need for change of direction, of behaviour and means in accordance with the person's lifepath and karma. From Saturn onwards, all planets have a strong karmic connotation.

Keep in mind essentially that Uranus can unexpectedly change the course of your life considerably with definitive consequences. It can create chaos as much as extraordinary success, depending on the rest of the chart at the time of the transit and on the level of evolution in the area affected by the transit.

Use the list of aphorisms below to guide your analyses of the transits of Uranus in each one of the twelve Houses. Once more, avoid copy-pasting those texts or taking them as a final product. Remember that the influence of a transits largely depends on what is happening in terms of other transits and of the general tendency of the birth chart, with particular attention to the natal position and "strength" of Uranus. Do not forget that freewill can overcome lots of obstacles and avoid many mishaps.

THE TRANSITS OF URANUS IN THE HOUSES

Alike Pluto and Neptune, the influence of transiting Uranus can last for many years in a House. It is more remarkable around the time when it enters or is close to the cusp of the House. Meanwhile, faster transits in conjunction with Uranus occasionally trigger its basic energy and role in the areas represented by the House concerned.

House I (Ascendant)
Great changes are to be expected in private life and personal needs and expectations with major outcomes in marriage and other important relationships due to the opposition formed with House VII. The areas represented by the House in Aquarius play a major role in the unfolding of exceptional events while the transit lasts, with greater emphasis around the time of the conjunction with the cusp of the Ascendant.

House II
Major events are likely to produce irreversible changes in material life. Food and finances take on a totally different path due to unexpected circumstances. The move may be work or health related. Financial status is submitted to the need to take on a completely new direction influenced by the opposition with House VIII. Inheritance, for example, is not unlikely. The areas represented by the House in Aquarius play an important role during this transit.

House III
The change produced by this transit involves intellectual and communication skills. Unexpected events may generate a complete transformation of the understanding of life and human interactions. Extraordinary thoughts and ideas may become a source of exceptional realisations. Long-distance travels and higher education needs are caused by the opposition of Uranus with House IX. The areas represented by the House in Aquarius play an important role during this transit.

House IV

Major changes are to be expected in relation to the place of residence and family environment. Career and social status are also concerned due to the opposition of Uranus with House X. Exceptional situations may produce a complete turn of fate with happy or unpleasant outcomes depending on other configurations occurring simultaneously. The areas represented by the House in Aquarius play an important role during this transit.

House V

This period coincides with major events involving love or loved-ones that produce exceptional and unexpected changes. A totally new way of life is motivated by an inner need for complete metamorphose. Creativity is also concerned. Unique realisations are likely, with drastic consequences in social surroundings, both human and geographical. The areas represented by the House in Aquarius play an important role during this transit.

House VI

Unexpected events may produce drastic changes in work related activities. Extraordinary circumstances motivate or force such transformations. Health can become a determining factor. New ideas inspired by unforeseen situations initiate a definitive turn of fate with unique repercussions on a higher level of consciousness through the opposition formed with House XII. The areas represented by the House in Aquarius play an important role during this transit.

House VII

This transit coincides with a period of complete and unexpected turn in major relationships such as marriage or professional partnership. The other person involved is marked by the influence of Uranus and may therefore become responsible for the change. A profound modification of the inner-self and personality is also observed. It is due to the opposition produced by Uranus with the Ascendant. The areas represented by the House in Aquarius play a major role during this transit.

House VIII

Unexpected events such as inheritance or some exceptional return on investment are likely to initiate crucial changes of situation with major financial repercussions. The main source of revenue is likely to be transformed by the influence of Uranus opposite House II. A new approach to the mysteries of life and death caused by extraordinary circumstances is also indicated. The areas represented by the House in Aquarius play an important role during this transit.

House IX

This period is marked by unexpected changes that deeply modify the intellectual and philosophical approach to life. There may be a change of circumstances derived from official or legal decisions. Long-distance travel, higher education and social ambitions are likely to motivate and produce some of the events generated by Uranus. The areas represented by the House in Aquarius play an important role during this transit.

House X (MC)

Uranus transiting here produces major changes that may affect both career orientation and social-professional status. Totally new projects and objectives emerge from unexpected events or opportunities with definitive consequences. New ideas and the ability to make use of elaborate tools with skill and originality favour a great turn of fate. The influence of Uranus is also predictable in the family and residential environment because of the opposition with House IV. The areas represented by the House in Aquarius play an important role during this transit.

House XI

This transit announces changes that are likely to have a definitive impact on social life and environment, both human and geographical. There may be a link with love, romance, creativity, or art, because of the opposition with House V. New friends and acquaintances favour a profound transformation of daily routine and habits. Unexpected encounters with determining consequences are indicated. The areas represented by the House in Aquarius also play a major role during this period.

House XII

The changes produced by Uranus have a deep spiritual or karmic connotation. This is a period of inner questioning and transformation. Unusual exceptional events trigger new feelings and a strong attraction to the more subtle plans of existence through astral travel and other types of extraordinary experiences. Work or health are also involved in the unfolding of events because of the opposition with House VI. The areas represented by the House in Aquarius play a major role during this transit.

Lesson 12

CHIRON

As seen earlier, Chiron takes around fifty years to complete a revolution of the zodiac. Trapped between Saturn and Uranus, Chiron is a sort of synthesis of the combined energies of the giant planets. The first one, Saturn, is Cronos: time, the past, difficulties and obstacles that enforce progress and determination. The second one, Uranus, represents the future and what is holds in terms of hopes and fears stemming from drastic unexpected changes.

Chiron, the thinker, the analyst, the sage, places itself as mediator of the perpetual combat between the past and the future. Its transits coincide with periods of enlightenment and revelation issued from the ability to accept and learn the lessons of life to progress in the areas represented by Chiron in the chart (House in Virgo and where Chiron was at birth).

Chiron comes back to its original position only once in a lifetime expect for those who live over a hundred years. The transits durations through the Houses vary greatly from one chart to another. If this is due to the eccentric orbit of Chiron as explained in chapter 4, it is also because of the size of the Houses.

The entry of Chiron in a House signals the beginning of a long period of reflexion during which it becomes necessary to take care of the area represented like a doctor would do after a medical check-up. Good health is the most precious possession. This is true physiologically, psychologically, and symbolically. When Chiron transits a House, it acts to treat and cure deficiencies in the areas represented by that House, but it can also confirm and preserve good health in the areas concerned.

Chiron's slow progression around the zodiac means that its influence is more remarkable when it makes a conjunction with the cusp of a House, but also when it enters the sign where the House stands. Observed the chart on the next page for a moment.

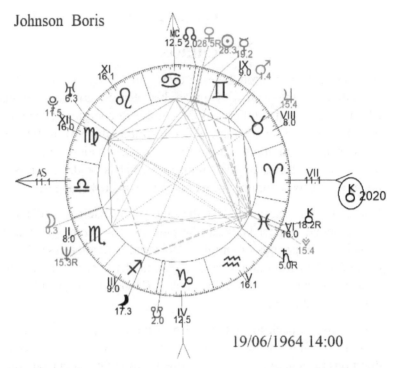

Johnson Boris

19/06/1964 14:00

In 2019, Boris Johnson becomes UK's prime Minister and succeed in getting his country out of the European Union. The Brexit shows how fragile the EU is and how many problems it is likely to face in the years to come.

In 2019, Chiron was in Aries, near the cusp of House VII in Boris Johnson's birth chart. Chiron's karmic meaning is applied to political alliances and personal relationships. That was a year when important partnerships led to victory. It is also the year when Boris and Carrie Symonds, a Pisces with the Moon also in Pisces, got engaged.

At the same time, Chiron was making an opposition with Mr Johnson's Ascendant in Libra. Health was to become an issue. More so because Chiron was transiting House VI (work and health). Chiron rules House XII (in Virgo) enhancing the karmic nature of the transit. House XII also represents what is hidden or not visible, like a virus for example… On March 17, 2020, while the Sun was forming a transiting conjunction with Chiron in Aries, the BBC news bulletin announces that the man had caught the COVID_19, a virus that did so many casualties and economic damage worldwide in 2020.[14] Quite energetic and combative, as well as treated with the best available medicine, the young man recovered quickly. However, no one knows how or for how long the after-effects of the disease may continue to bother him. Chiron will transit in Aries until April 15, 2027…

Apart from the notion of health as such, the transits of Chiron coincide with periods during which the need to analyse, reflex, and ponder can become as much as a vital necessity in order to learn from passed mistakes and to assume the consequences in the areas represented by the Houses concerned.

Chiron is the "inner doctor" who confers the ability to self-healing. It acts on the immune system, both physiologically and psychologically. By blending this natural talent with the ability to think and analyse, Chiron's influence becomes an important factor of strength to fight illnesses as such, and all sorts of other disorders, be them social, professional, personal, or familial, and find efficient rational solutions or cures.

Next, you will find a list of aphorisms to help you analyse the transits of Chiron. Again, I repeat that those short texts are only meant as a guide. They are not to be used direct from the book to explain wisely and successfully the influence of Chiron. Remember that a transit NEVER ACTS ALONE.

---

[14] Watch the video about 2020 that I made in July 2019, announcing a historical year: https://www.youtube.com/watch?v=gDaZZkVrM4s

THE TRANSITS OF CHIRON IN THE HOUSES

House I (Ascendant)
This transit indicates a long period of inner questioning and self-analysis to answer this fundamental question: "who am I?" A strong need to be someone enhances the ability to heal by understanding why and how inner and outer selves should cohabit to become a real person instead of a human puppet pulled apart between the desire to be and the uncertainty of being alive. The areas represented by the House in Virgo play an important role during this transit.

House II
This is an important period of reflexion and analysis of the reality of life on a material point of view. It coincides with a need to observe culinary rules to preserve or restore a healthy body. The main source of revenue is subject to self-criticism and inner evaluation. The result can be a complete professional restructuration to heal what is considered unfit and unfavourable to carry on. The areas represented by the House in Virgo play an important role during this transit.

House III
Inner questioning and self-criticism become a necessary "headache" to strengthen the intellect and mental awareness. Useful in periods of studies, Chiron favours sophisticated mental activity and better attention to details. There may be a difficult situation involving siblings or a karmic encounter while travelling. Self-consciousness may contribute to intellectual uneasiness. The areas represented by the House in Virgo play an important role during this transit.

House IV
Family affairs and home environment are subject to a more complex approach and management due to unforeseen difficult or unfortunate circumstances. Chiron accentuates the health-factor issued from a family member's illness. However, it confers a rational attitude to deal with existential challenges of karmic nature. The ability to focus on details helps find appropriate solutions. The areas represented by the House in Virgo play an important role during this transit.

House V

Chiron here indicates that love, romance, and relationships with loved ones are likely to become a source of karmic difficulties. The need to understand produces intense questioning to determine why such hurdles happen and how they can be utilized to progress morally and spiritually. This period can also be marked by the illness of a child, or a sentimental or artistic struggle. The areas represented by the House in Virgo play an important role during this transit.

House VI

Chiron is in its "natural House of rulership"[15] where its influence implies health and work more directly. This transit corresponds to a period during which a more complex and detailed approach is needed either to treat a worrying health condition or to find rational solutions to professional situations. Incidents involving domestic animals are likely. The areas represented by the House in Virgo play an important role during this transit.

House VII

This transit corresponds to a long period of test and challenge in personal relationships and other important social or professional partnerships. There is a need to analyse and reflect on the karmic nature of human interactions with the purpose of understanding why and how life has led to the situation that has developed prior to this transit. The areas represented by the House in Virgo play an important role during this period.

House VIII

Chiron here emphasizes the need to accept the end philosophically rather than as a fatality, but it helps understand what needs to be done to stay alive longer. It may also enhance nihilistic tendencies by suggesting that money and earthly possessions should not be a source of constraints and limitations, but simply parts of a whole that includes more subtle non-material values. The areas represented by the House in Virgo play an important role during this transit.

---

[15] Chiron rules the sixth sign, Virgo. It is therefore also the symbolic ruler of the sixth House, no matter in what sign it is.

House IX

In this House, Chiron has a strong influence as it imposes a profound reflexion and evaluation of the philosophical meaning of life. It may also accentuate the degree of human interaction on legal, administrative, and official matters. The need or desire to study, travel and derive greater returns from intellectual work is also enhanced. The areas represented by the House in Virgo play an important role during this transit.

House X (MC)

Chiron here emphasises the need for a careful evaluation of the meaning of success as seen through formal education and family background. To come to term with personal ambitions and choose the best possible tools to reach important goals are essentials to avoid climbing toward the wrong summit. Health, real or symbolic, is part of the issues to resolve. The areas represented by the House in Virgo play an important role during this transit.

House XI

This period is marked by a need to reflect on the reality of life when it comes to friendship, social standing, and environment, both human and geographical. Karmic encounters produce unusual situations. Difficulties are as source of motivation. Health is a factor of interrogations motivating formal or personal studies to understand causes and heal their detrimental effects. The areas represented by the House in Virgo play an important role during this transit.

House XII

This transit in the most spiritual House of all gives Chiron an important role as leader of the search for inner truth in relation to passed events, situations, and motivations. Health may play a dominant part in the connexion between earthly and heavenly realty. A need for introspection is observed. It is advised to exteriorise anger or resentment to avoid somatisation. The areas represented by the House in Virgo play a major role during this transit.

* * * * * * * * *

Remember how the duration of Chiron's transit is different from one area of the zodiac to another. This is due to its eccentric orbit. As long as it remains in a House, the work to be done is dealing with the difficulties knowing that various forms of enrichment always stem from the efforts we make. Chiron does not "let go" easily. This mythological entity waited until the very last struggle to heal from its wound before accepting to exchange its immortality and die.

Chiron represents the sense of personal sacrifice to find peace at he highest spiritual level. Through its great suffering, Chiron understood that death was an open door to another life. The question is: will it be better or worse than this one?"…

In Boris Johnson's chart, Chiron in in Aries. The energy of this sign is combative and intense. It is an asset to fight health issues and other important problems. It also shows that his life is far from ending yet. There are still many years for him to dwell on the affairs of his country, either as PM or in any other way.

Lesson 13

SATURN

Saturn, two and a half times slower than Jupiter, but around three times faster than Uranus does not represent enthusiasm and happiness. Unlike Jupiter with its strong aura of evolution and success, Saturn does not either produce drastic and unexpected changes like Uranus can. However, the transits of Saturn allow concrete realisations with long-lasting repercussions in the areas of life represented by the House in Capricorn and the House transited by this planet.

Saturn represents accomplishment. It indicates how efforts are rewarded and how strongly they influence the degree of sustained energy to reach the most important goals and surmount the highest obstacles. It also represents "imminent karma". With Saturn, if nothing is done, nothing is gained.

Saturn is the schoolteacher who imposes homework and various obligations. The dedicated students are assured to gain their teacher's good will and to succeed at examinations. Their future is likely to be more gratifying. On the contrary, the idle students attract negative reactions that can greatly alter their ability to academically succeed. Of course, it is not all black or white, there are many shades of grey that need to be addressed to get a more subtle and precise information from the position of Saturn in a chart and while it transits around it.

Saturn has a bad reputation. Its transits are too often considered negatively. Saturn frightens. It is however a most interesting planet with a karmic aura linked to the principle of cause and effect. Saturn is traditionally categorised as a "maleficent" planet, together with Mars and Pluto. It is true that the karmic nature of its influence can coincide with very difficult periods. Natural disasters and catastrophes, pandemics and long-lasting economic recessions are often linked to a transit of Saturn. However, by itself, the energy of this planet is not sufficient to become prejudicial to this kind of extreme outcome.

The great conjunction of 2020 in Capricorn involving Jupiter, Saturn and Pluto was the first occurrence in 6,594 years! To me, it was evident that it announced a very unique year, historical and somewhat hysterical too!

That said, I invite you not to forecast the worse because of a discordant transit of Saturn. As I constantly repeat to my students, Saturn will be on your side from the moment you consider it as an ally rather than an enemy. Saturn is time (Cronos). It teaches patience and determination that build up endurance and resilience, essential qualities to succeed durably.

Saturn shows us that speeding is a source of incidents, errors, and other unpleasant outcomes. Being too slow is just as disadvantageous to our projects because it deters our ability to be where we need to be, say what we need to say, and do what we need to do when the time is right. The three W's: **w**here, **w**hat, and **w**hen must closely collaborate to ensure success. Timing is often difficult to determine. Astrology is the tool to do so efficiently. I hope this book helps you decide on the best possible moments to make important decisions by observing and analysing the effects of the transits around your birth chart or anybody else's…

Next is a list of aphorisms to help you analyse the transits of Saturn in the Houses. I do not need to repeat that those texts are only a glimpse of how much valuable information can be derived from the voyage of Saturn through the Houses and the signs where they stand. Use your own word and let yourself be inspired by the transcending energy of the great master of time.

THE TRANSITS OF SATURN IN THE HOUSES

House I (Ascendant)

Saturn here signifies maturation and affirmation of the self. Difficulties demand effort and determination to overcome obstacles and obtain long-lasting positive results. Depending on age, Saturn's transit may be linked to events and experiences dating back to around thirty years. The potential to succeed durably depends on the amount of work done while Saturn transited in House XII. The areas represented by the House in Capricorn play an important role during this transit.

House II

This is a period of maturation regarding money and food. There may be a degree on dissatisfaction due to financial difficulties and a tendency to negatively deal with the material aspect of life. However, Saturn can also coincide with a time of concrete long-lasting realisations. Its influence enhances the karmic nature of the situation. It emphasises reality in a down-to-earth manner that cannot be ignored. The areas represented by the House in Capricorn play an important role during this transit.

House III

Saturn here provides intellectual maturation through difficult experiences requiring extra mental effort to deal with challenges fruitfully. This period may be marked by an involvement in studies or by a karmic situation involving siblings. Communication can be a source of dissatisfaction and limitation. The amount of work done to beat negative thinking strengthens self-confidence and the potential to succeed. The areas represented by the House in Capricorn play an important role during this transit.

House IV

This transit coincides with a period of residential or family affirmation and realisation. The time factor intervenes primarily in the unfolding of events leading to concrete achievement. The karmic nature of the planet can put pressure on close environment and force extra effort to deal with difficulties effectively. Saturn-produced unfortunate events build up strength by imposing extra effort to overcome obstacles. The areas represented by the House in Capricorn play an important role during this transit.

House V

This is a period of maturation regarding the expression of love and the evolution of creativity. At the same time, difficulties are likely to create a negative approach to intimate relationships. Extra effort is required to derive concrete benefit from unfortunate experiences. The karmic nature of the planet shows how important love is to overcome obstacles. Childhood becomes a source of valuable information. The areas represented by the House in Capricorn play an important role during this transit.

House VI

This transit coincides with a period of concretisation at work with long-lasting repercussions. It allows maturation through passed experiences and the effort made to overcome difficulties. Saturn can however slow down the process of evolution due to unemployment or challenging health disorder. If there was a previous transit thirty years before, it may be a source of valuable information to better understand this one. The areas represented by the House in Capricorn play a major role during this transit.

House VII

This transit corresponds to a period of tests and realisations in important relationships. Realities need to be addressed with pragmatism and patience. Difficulties emphasise the necessity to collaborate in a more mature manner with partners or associates, both socially and privately. The karmic nature of Saturn can be a source of misfortune from which lessons and experiences become a concrete source of personal evolution. The areas represented by the House in Capricorn play a major role during this transit.

House VIII

This transit produces important events that profoundly affect personal behaviour with its influence in finances and earthly possessions. Time and patience are necessary to deal with delays and material hardship or loss. The notion of death, really or symbolically, emanates from the need to regenerate with more maturity and efficiency. The karmic nature of Saturn confers a more meaningful aura to unfortunate events. The areas represented by the House in Capricorn play a major role during this transit.

House IX
Life is philosophically subjected to a series of karmic tests that make this transit a most important journey in terms of maturity and intellectual, or moral evolution. This period can be marked by the obtention of a major diploma or other official recognition. Saturn can also help concretise long distance travels and their incidence in various sectors of life. Saturn has much to teach in terms of existential realities. The areas represented by the House in Capricorn play a major role during this transit.

House X (MC)
Saturn is the natural ruler of this House which is symbolically linked to the tenth sign: Capricorn. The transit corresponds to a major period of social and professional realisation. What is organised and achieved is likely to have long-lasting repercussions until the next transit in thirty years' time. It is also a period to make major decisions about the home and family situation through the opposition with House IV. The areas represented by the House in Capricorn play a major role during this transit.

House XI
This transit is likely to produce karmic encounters, intense human relations, and challenging social situations. Friendship may become a source of difficulties and dissatisfaction, but it can also motivate and favour concrete realisations. What happened when Saturn was in House X weighs heavily during this one. The past is to be taken into consideration to avoid mistakes and their unfortunate consequences. The areas represented by the House in Capricorn play a major role during this transit.

House XII

When a karmic planet visits a karmic House, the transit promises to be quite challenging and revealing of far-distant past realities that must be confronted and overcome. Saturn here confers a strong need to confront hardship with patience and determination. It is a period of gestation during which what is done will be a source of concrete realisation when the planet journeys through the following House. The areas represented by the House in Capricorn play a major role during this transit.

Lesson 14

JUPITER

Jupiter travels an average of one year in each sign. It can remain up to twelve days around the same degree of the zodiac. Years of practice have showed me that the influence of Jupiter is felt up to one month before the exact conjunction with the cusp of a House. In the case of a double or triple transit, due to retrogradations, the energy of the giant planet is naturally more intense and durable. In that case, the first occurrence, when the planet is in direct motion, represents the moment to choose to "plant a seed" or to initiate a project. The second occurrence, when it retrogrades, is comparable to the germination stage. The third and last occurrence, when Jupiter is in direct motion again, is equivalent to the time of harvesting and reaping of the rewards.

Jupiter is considered as mostly beneficial, but other transits occurring simultaneously must be analysed to make a more accurate prognosis. Jupiter transfers the expansion principle to the areas represented by the House transited. It can produce a tendency to exaggerate and show too much enthusiasm and not enough caution. Errors and other incongruities are therefore likely to occur.

We know that too much exposure to the Sun produces burns and other painful reactions. The effect of Jupiter is similar in an intangible way. A transit in a House can last up to two years or more, depending on its size. During such a long journey, Jupiter's radiations penetrate deeply and can produce major outcomes, beneficial or detrimental, depending on other transits that may significantly modify Jupiter's basic impact.

In 2016, for example, Jupiter was in Virgo while Saturn transited in Sagittarius and Neptune in Pisces. The three giant planets were in discordance, affecting each other with important consequences in the areas represented by the Houses concerned in a birth chart. These are the Houses in Sagittarius, Capricorn and Pisces ruled by each planet, and the House where the three were transiting…

To me, the incidence of Jupiter in a House begins as soon as the planet enters the sign where it stands. The farther the cusp of the House is, the longer Jupiter takes to reach it. That time should be used to prepare for the concretisation of the effect of the transit in the areas of life represented by the House in question. Periods of retrogradation must also be taken into consideration. And then, when Jupiter effectively transits that House, it will leave the sign where the House begins to transit the following one. That is when its influence gets ready for the next House, wherever its cusp is in the sign. See the chart below to visualise this concept.

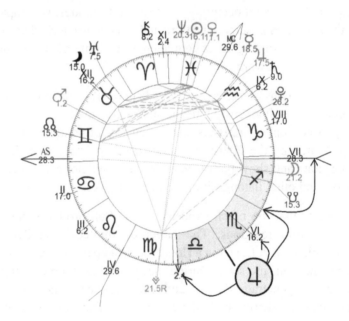

Jupiter is transiting House V. As it enters Scorpio, still in House V, it begins to influence House VI. Later, when it enters Sagittarius, still in House VI, it begins to influence House VII. The same procedure applies to the following signs and Houses.

THE TRANSITS OF JUPITER IN THE HOUSES

House I (Ascendant)

This is a period of evolution of the need for more authenticity in the expression of the self. Charm and charisma are enhanced. They are likely to favour projects in profound affinity with the innate talents and other natural abilities. Jupiter can also produce various excesses derived from exaggerated opportunism with detrimental incidence in personal relationships. The areas represented by the House in Sagittarius play an important role during this transit.

House II

This period is likely to be marked by an evolution of the potential to earn money and to enjoy earthly benefits on a material point of view. A stronger attraction to the good things of life may produce weight gain or digestive discomfort. However, this is a period to choose to request a wage rise or to invest on a six-year term project and rip the benefit when Jupiter transits House VIII. The areas represented by the House in Sagittarius play an important role during this transit.

House III

Jupiter increases the need to communicate, to travel, to move, and to meet people more spontaneously. It favours neurons production and cerebral vivacity. It therefore enhances intellectual potentials, with positive effects on more complex mental processes. This is a period to choose to enrol in a course of studies to improve personal knowledge or professional avenues. The areas represented by the House in Sagittarius play an important role during this transit.

House IV

This period is marked by a degree of evolution in the family and home environment. It may be linked to the birth of a sibling or to the realisation of an important project concerning the place of residence. However, Jupiter can also produce excessive enthusiasm and a tendency to get involved in expensive projects. Caution is advised to avoid resulting difficulty and concern. The areas represented by the House in Sagittarius play an important role during this transit.

House V

This transit increases both creative and procreative potentials. It is favourable to artists and children who seem to progress remarkably under the generous influence of Jupiter. This period may be marked by and evolution of the romantic aspect of life. Jupiter enhances personal charm and charisma, luck, and the joy of being alive. Excessive optimism is however likely. The areas represented by the House in Sagittarius play an important role during this transit.

House VI

Work and health are primarily affected by the powerful influence of Jupiter. Professional evolution is likely. Jupiter boosts vital energy, both physiologically and psychologically. A more positive approach to health issues allows for quicker recovery. However, excessive optimism may increase the number of tasks to complete with negative effect on moral and physical balance. The areas represented by the House in Sagittarius play an important role during this transit.

House VII

An important relationship or partnership such as marriage or other private or professional alliance is likely to officially take place. There is a genuine desire and potential to increase human interaction motivated by an opportunity to participate in a joint venture with great prospective. However, excessive enthusiasm and trust need to be controlled to avoid disappointment. The areas represented by the House in Sagittarius play an important role during this transit.

House VIII

An important financial transaction may significantly improve the material aspect of social life. It can be inheritance, real estate, return on investment or other event of great importance involving earthly possessions or acquisitions. Sexual needs are also stronger. Jupiter enhances the potential to regenerate or heal from illness or other existential setbacks. The areas represented by the House in Sagittarius play an important role during this transit.

House IX

This is Jupiter's natural House of rulership where its influence is stronger and more remarkable. Legal affairs, higher studies, long-distance travels, and formal aspects of social life are affected. Before House X, where it enhances the potential to succeed, this transit corresponds to a period of active preparation and organisation to obtain better results from the next House. The areas represented by the House in Sagittarius play an important role during this transit.

House X (MC)

Jupiter announces a period of evolution of the career or professional status. It coincides with opportunities to progress up the social ladder. Advancement or accession to a higher level of responsibilities is likely to be a source of great personal satisfaction. The opposition to House IV can however indicate some difficulty to harmoniously blend family affairs and personal ambitions. The areas represented by the House in Sagittarius play an important role during this transit.

House XI

This period is marked by a potential evolution of social relationships, either in number or in the quality. Generosity towards the community contributes to popularity and success. Acquaintances and opportunistic encounters enhance the potential to greatly improve life in various ways. However, excessive optimism or trust in others may be a source of disappointment. The areas represented by the House in Sagittarius play an important role during this transit.

House XII

This transit announces a period of preparation or "gestation" to Jupiter's journey through the Ascendant where it has a remarkable influence. There may be a need for introspection and a link with past events dating back to one of the previous occurrences, at least twelve years before. Latent discontent can become more obvious and troubling through psychosomatic distress. The areas represented by the House in Sagittarius play an important role during this transit.

Lessons 15

THE FASTER TRANSITS
From Vesta to the Moon

VESTA

Vesta is the slowest in the category of fast planets. In ancient Roman traditions, Vesta was the symbol of the city's harmony and balance. The temple of Vesta was guarded and looked after by seven virgins, symbol of Virgo. Their main task was to protect the divinely reproduction of a phallus, symbol of Scorpio. Libra, the seventh sign, placed between Virgo and Scorpio, is therefore quite in resonance with the myth of Vesta. That is why I have adopted it to represents this sign.

Vesta is what astronomers call a "planetoid" or "asteroid". It orbits at an average 353 million kilometres around the Sun between Mars and Jupiter in three years and ten months. It is the third largest asteroid (diameter 390 km) after Ceres (diameter 1,300 km) and Pallas (diameter 550 km). Here is part of an article published in 1983 in the Encyclopedia Britannica's scientific section:

"Vesta (minor planet), the brighter of all minor planets, although one of the smallest, and the only one in its category to be visible to the naked eye. It was the fourth minor planet to be discovered on March 29, 1807 by Henrich Wilhelm Matthäus Olbers. Its diameter is of 390 km. The reason to its brightness in unknown.[16]"

---

[16] Vesta is unique among asteroids in that it has light and dark patches on the surface, much like the moon. Ground-based observations determined that the asteroid has basaltic regions, meaning that lava once flowed across its surface.

I use Vesta as Libra's ruler since 1998. I invite you to verify its influence according to the House in Libra, to the position of Vesta in sign and House, and to the aspects formed with other elements in the chart. You should soon recognise its role as ruler of the seventh sign…

THE ROLE OF THE FASTER TRANSITS

If the slow transits act in a profound long-lasting manner, the faster ones are often useful to the slower ones to reveal their latent influence in the areas represented by the Houses concerned.

However, a fast planet has a personal influence that is punctually observed while it transits a House. Vesta is no exception. With a journey of around 110 days through a sign, its influence does not need any other to express itself quite remarkably. Vesta brings harmony and balance in the areas represented by the Houses concerned during its transits. Its influence begins as soon as it enters the sign in which a House stands, while continuing to act on the House where it is still transiting. See the example chart on the following page to understand what I mean.

During its transit in a House, the energy of Vesta is appeasing and harmonising. It helps balance things out and avoid extreme reactions in case of a conflict or other unexpected event or incident. Its role is discreet and subtly beneficial. A feeling of wellbeing ensues, together with a degree of improvement in the areas represented by the House concerned.

Its action on slower transits can accentuate their role in a favourable way, while diminishing the incidence of difficult ones. For example, when Vesta conjuncts transiting Jupiter, its beneficial influence is strengthened, more noticeable, and spontaneously exploitable. When Vesta conjuncts transiting Saturn, it tempers the constraints it represents, and makes reality less detrimental or difficult to confront.

Do not forget the rule often repeated in this book: "a transit never acts alone." Blending various influences is the key to a proper, tangible, and useful forecast.

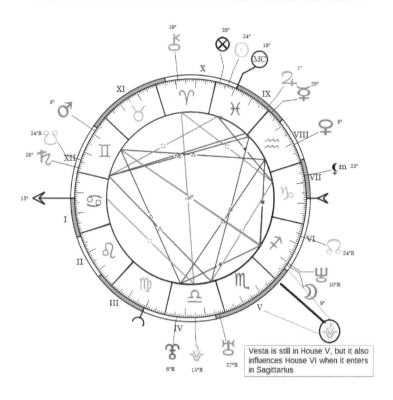

Vesta is still in House V, but it also influences House VI when it enters in Sagittarius

In 2020, transiting Jupiter, Saturn, and Pluto were conjunct in Capricorn. If each planet's influence is analysed separately, the information derived would be very limited. Blending all three together allows a more comprehensive and realistic reading. This conjunction made the historical year we all had to live through. Millions lost the battle and died from the Covid19 infection, not mentioning the millions deeply harmed by the economic consequences of the pandemic…

Next, you will find a series of short aphorisms to describe the potential influence of transiting Vesta in each one of the twelve Houses. The texts include, but without openly mentioning it, the incidence of each transit on the opposite House.

THE TRANSITS OF VESTA IN THE HOUSES

House I (Ascendant)

Whatever may be detrimental to inner wellbeing is counteracted by the appeasing energy of Vesta. It has a positive influence that enhances personal talents and potentials in a subtle and well-balanced manner. The search for the middle way is favoured by inspiring thoughts and perspectives. The areas represented by the House in Libra play an important soothing role during this transit.

House II

Vesta has a beneficial effect on finances, revenues, and other aspects of material life. Food and dietetics are also favoured. The assimilation process is more efficient, with positive aftereffects. Earthly values and possessions, artistic traits, or creativity are sources of motivation and wellbeing. The areas represented by the House in Libra may play an interesting role during this transit.

House III

This period is marked by a more effective handling of human relationships and mental interactions. Vesta calms and appeases mind and spirit. It favours learning and communicating. Interesting encounters during short trips are likely. They have a soothing effect and may become a source of positive motivation. Relations with siblings are enhanced and harmonised. The areas represented by the House in Libra may play a dominant role during this transit.

House IV

Home life and familial relationships are easier, harmonised, and a source of satisfaction. Vesta helps solve eventual problems more effectively. Tensions tend to disappear. Arguments between siblings are less likely. There is a need for peace and quiet that improves the quality of life in the place of residence and immediate surroundings. The areas represented by the House in Libra plays an important role during this period depending on other simultaneous transits.

House V

Love life and creativity benefit from the soothing, harmonising influence of Vesta. Simple enjoyment and intimate pleasure are a source of positive motivation and inner satisfaction. Children participate in a nicer way to the better moments in life. Artistic activity is favoured by inspiration and a more sensible approach or style. The areas represented by the House in Libra play an important role during this transit.

House VI

Work and health usually benefit from the soothing and balancing influence of Vesta passing through this House. In case of an illness, medical treatment is more effective. Professional activities and interactions are easier to manage. They are a source of positive motivation and results. The ability to harmonise diverging opinions improves both production and human relationships. The areas linked to the House in Libra may play a dominant role during this transit.

House VII

Partnerships are made easier by the effect of Vesta in its House of "natural rulership" where it is stronger and more efficient. Marriage and other major relationships are often subject to fluctuations due to various differences between the persons involved. The ability to solve major problems is greatly enhanced by Vesta's journey through this House with good results. The areas represented by the House in Libra have an important role to play during this transit.

House VIII

This may be an auspicious period to invest money, to conduct an important financial transaction, to contact the bank for a loan, or to benefit from some form of material or spiritual inheritance. Sexuality is enhanced in a harmonious way. The interest in the mysteries of life and death is increased. The potential to regenerate is improved and favours natural healing. The areas represented by the House in Libra play a major role during this transit.

House IX

Some degree of satisfaction is to be expected in all official dealings. While studying, the influence of Vesta increases the ability to understand and to do the mental work required. While travelling, Vesta produces pleasant moments and situations. This period is also marked by a more philosophical approach to life's circumstances with positive outcomes in case of trouble. The areas represented by the House in Libra may play an advantageous role during this transit.

House X (MC)

This period is marked by an evolution of the potential to reach higher levels of achievement at work or in the realisation of important projects. Harmonious relations with superiors or clients favour the emergence of opportunities and potential career evolution. A positive approach to existential difficulties simplifies the process of finding appropriate solutions. The areas represented by the House in Libra may play an important role during this transit.

House XI

Satisfactions are to be expected from social life, friendship, and human or geographical environment. Vesta makes it easier to relate to other people, to converse and to spend enjoyable time in various collective activities. What is done for others with authentic and spontaneous generosity is a source of personal satisfaction while it increases popularity and opportunities. The areas represented by the House in Libra play an important role during this transit.

House XII

The past may become a source of pleasant surprises through interesting events or situations arousing fond memories of a person, place, event, or situation. The natural connexion with the spiritual dimension of life is intensified with soothing and appeasing effects. Vesta also enhances the natural ability to self-healing in various ways, depending on the problems to solve. The areas represented by the House in Libra play an important role during this transit.

Lesson 16

MARS

The transits of Mars are faster than any of those mentioned from the beginning of this book. As such, Mars has a strong triggering effect on the latent influence of slower planets. They are always more remarkable when they involve the sign, or the House ruled by the slower transiting planet. For example, Jupiter transiting in House III in Sagittarius is likely to be more effective than in any other sign. This is even greater if Jupiter transits House IX in Sagittarius. In both cases, the Houses concerned are subject to a more considerable force that enhances the potential to progress and succeed in the areas of life concerned with long-lasting repercussions due to the time Jupiter takes to complete a revolution of the zodiac (almost twelve years). It happens that a situation or event taking place during a transit of Jupiter in a House produces repercussions twelve years later, when the transit occurs again.

The transits of Mars increase the importance of the areas represented by the House concerned. The moment Mars conjuncts the cusp of a House is critical in terms of what it can produce in the areas represented by that House. It is therefore important to follow Mars around the zodiac to forecast these important occurrences and deal with their possible consequences more effectively. Mars can increase impulsiveness, reactivity, and combativity with disrupting consequences. It confers more stamina to act and react, but its energy needs to be channelled and controlled to avoid mishaps…

Using the ephemerides, go back in time approximately one year or so, and try to remember what happened when Mars formed transiting conjunctions or near conjunctions with certain House cusps in your birth chart. You should quickly understand how powerful the influence of this planet to trigger quick happening events and intense situations. Do not panic, though, Mars can be extremely positive and favourable to effective action in many ways, physically, mentally, and otherwise. It all depends on the "nature of Mars" in a birth chart. The configurations involving it with other planets and elements play a major role to determine if Mars is beneficial or detrimental in a chart. Besides this investigation, the transiting aspects produced by Mars with other transiting planets help determine the nature of the influence. Mars mostly accentuates combativity. It is a useful and even necessary quality. It can, however, get out of hands and become destructive rather than the contrary. Blending and synthesising all transiting configurations involving Mars is a must to obtain a proper reading and a realistic prognosis.

When Mars comes back to its original position in a chart, the event corresponds to the end of a two-year cycle of actions and reactions of mixed consequences. The return of Mars is a moment to choose to ponder and reflect on the two-year past. Doing this allows better control of the psychological and physical influence of Mars to make it more efficient instead of repeating the same type of behaviour and mistakes again. Well above its "fortune-telling" use and abuse, astrology is before all a fabulous self-development tool.

Mars remains an average of six weeks in a sign. A House can be much larger than a sign. This means that Mars can play a role in the areas represented for a longer period. When Mars retrogrades, it is likely to be retained within the same area of the zodiac, if not the same sign, for up to six months. That is what happened in 2020 when Mars transited in Aries between 28 June 2020 and 6 January 2021. The longer the transit, the more "damage" it can do, but it also allows better adaptation to and better control of its influence.

Next you will find a series of twelve aphorisms to guide your analysis of the transit of Mars in each House. They may be useful to inspire your reading if, as explained each time, you do not take them for granted.

THE TRANSITS OF MARS IN THE HOUSES

House I (Ascendant)
There is an increase in reactivity especially in private life, except if the Ascendant and the Sun sign are the same. The intensity may be difficult to control to avoid various conflicts in partnerships linked to House VII opposed to the Ascendant. Self-consciousness is increased and becomes a source of greater determination causing inner tensions and occasional headaches. The areas represented by the House in Aries play a major role during this transit.

House II
There is a tendency to impulsive spending that may be a source of errors and tension in finances and budget keeping. Mars is likely to increase the need to defend and protect material possessions. Food can also become a source of renewed motivation and interest in dietetic. Important decisions involving money have to be taken prudently rather than impetuously. The areas represented by the House in Aries play a major role during this transit.

House III
Speeding increases the risk of accidents while driving. Mars here produces a tendency to argue and react aggressively. Moving, walking, or travelling may become a source of unpleasant events and incidents. Assertive or vindictive behaviour increases the ability to impose personal ideas and concepts, but it also creates discords that temper the potential to succeed wisely. The areas represented by the House in Aries play an important role during this transit.

House IV
This period is often marked by tensions due to important projects or situations involving the home and family. There may be significant work to be done around the place of residence. If so, care should be taken to avoid incidents or accidents while using tools and other potentially dangerous utensils. Domestic turbulences and accidents are possible due to accrued obligations and duties. The areas represented by the House in Aries play a major role during this transit.

House V

Mars intensifies the need to act and react with or about loved ones. Sentimental life may become turbulent. Love at first sight is often linked to this type of transit. Creativity is spontaneously and impulsively enhanced. The urge to satisfy personal desires creates inner tension and disruptions in personal relationship where jealousy is more apparent and distressing. The areas represented by the House in Aries play a major role during this transit.

House VI

More physical and mental energy increases the potential to work hard with stronger will and determination. It can also produce tensions with co-workers, errors, or incidents due to lack of patience and compassion. Daily home duties and responsibilities, or domestic animals are a source of accrued concern. In case of an illness, health may deteriorate sharply and recover quickly. The areas represented by the House in Aries play a major role during this transit.

House VII

The need to be more active in personal relationships or other important partnerships may become a source of accrued motivation and positive results if the energy is controlled and channelled to avoid unpleasant tensions. The ability to express personal needs peacefully rather than aggressively makes all the difference between avoiding or creating conflicts. The areas represented by the House in Aries plays a major role during this transit.

House VIII

During this period, Mars produces an increase in physical and sexual needs that may become a source of tension in close relationships. Financial interests are intensified and can create unwise investments decided impulsively, and conflicts with financial institutions. It is advised to avoid taking radical positions to manage corporate or family owned material assets. The areas represented by the House in Aries play an important role during this transit.

House IX

This period is marked by a proclivity to argument and debate about ethics, legal matters, long-distance travels, foreign countries, higher education, and philosophy. There is an urge to defend personal ideas passionately. Important decisions need to be patiently prepared to avoid errors and unpleasant incidents. Caution is advised about local regulations if travelling overseas. The areas represented by the House in Aries play a major role during this transit.

House X (MC)

Personal ambitions are a greater source of motivation when Mars journeys through the MC. It is useful to climb up the professional ladder. It may also render more aggressive and reactive with detrimental results and consequences. Career-related duties produce tension at home due to the opposition with House IV. However, hard work promotes success and progress. The areas of life represented by the House in Aries play a major role during this transit.

House XI

This period is marked by a greater implication or involvement in community work, social action, and occupations with friends. There could be tensions and arguments due to a tendency to lose patience quickly. Caution is recommended in physical activities and exercise to avoid accidents. The influence of the group may interfere with the expression of personal feelings in privacy. The areas represented by the House in Aries play a major role during this transit.

House XII

The past becomes a source of suppressed tension and a tendency to worry about events and situations dating back a long time. An effort is advised to avoid inner turmoil that could create irrational fears. This period prepares for the transit of Mars in the Ascendant. Being more open and spontaneous about personal issues helps find outside answers to troubling existential questions. The areas represented by the House in Aries play a major role during this transit.

Lesson 17

VENUS

The transits of Venus are usually quite beneficial. They act on personal magnetism and behaviour in the areas represented by the House concerned. The "radical" (original) position of Venus in a birth chart informs on the potential of its influence during its transits around the chart. The "stronger" the better without doubt. Venus is strong in Taurus and Libra and when it is in the Ascendant or Mid-Heaven. It is strong when it forms a conjunction with Jupiter or the Sun. It is strong when it is the dominant planet of the chart.

Alike Mercury, Venus is never far from the Sun in a chart. You will never find a square, trine, inconjunct, or opposition Sun/Venus or Sun/Mercury. Mercury and Venus are called "inferior planets" because they are closer to the Sun than the Earth. Hence, when looking at Venus or Mercury, we also look toward the Sun. Venus is the second planet from the Sun. Mercury is the first and closest. The Earth is number 3.

Venus is the goddess of love. It represents the good and beautiful things of life. When it transits a House, it improved the atmosphere and the energy in the areas represented by that House.

The transits of Venus through a sign last an average of three weeks. However, due to frequent retrogradations, Venus can be retained up to four months in the same sector of the zodiac, either in one sign, or between two signs. For example, from 5 November 2021, Venus transits in Capricorn. It goes into apparent retrogradation on 20 December at 26°29' in Capricorn. It resumes direct motion on 30 January 2022 at 11°05' in Capricorn. Finally, on 6 March 2022 it leaves that sign to transit in Aquarius. In all, Venus' journey in

Capricorn lasted four months. In 2020, a similar phenomenon occurred in Gemini, between 4 April and 4 August.

The transits of Venus are particularly interesting and beneficial when the planet transits the Sun sign. Those born under such sign are privileged by the duration of the transit. Except perhaps during the retrogradation period.

Next is a list of short aphorisms to help you along. Once again, they are not to be used as a final product. As explained for all the other planets analysed in this book, the influence of Venus greatly depends on other transits occurring concurrently.

THE TRANSITS OF VENUS IN THE HOUSES

In House I (Ascendant)

Venus here enhances personal vibration and charisma. It has a positive effect on the expression of inner personality. It improves self-confidence and self-esteem. It makes it possible to obtain privileges and other benefits from various sources. Luck seems more apparent and helpful in many ways. The areas represented by the House in Taurus play an important role during this transit.

In House II

This period is likely to be marked by financial improvement. A wage rise or other source of revenue may become a source of satisfaction. There is a stronger attraction to the earthly pleasures that could trigger weight gain due to excessive need to enjoy the simple pleasures of life in good company. The areas represented by the House in Taurus play an important role during this transit.

In House III

Communication skills are improved by the beneficial influence of Venus. Writers and other artists are more inspired and creative. Venus softens the manner of expression and favours diplomacy rather than force to impose personal thoughts and ideas. Enjoyable moments while travelling are also foreseeable. The areas represented by the House in Taurus play an important role during this transit.

In House IV

Home life and family relationships are improved by the beneficial influence of Venus. Decoration, creativity, love, affection, and compassion favour the emergence of various happy and enjoyable moments involving siblings and loved-ones. Projects and situation relating to the place of residence are favoured. The areas represented by the House in Taurus play an important role during this transit.

In House V

This is a period to choose to take a holiday and enjoy the good things of life. It is favourable to an involvement in a romantic relationship. The luck factor is enhanced in various ways. Personal charm and appeal are also increased. Artists benefit from greater creativity and inspiration. The areas represented by the House in Taurus play an important role during this transit.

In House VI

This period is likely to be marked by some improvement at work. More opportunities are indicated with beneficial outcomes. In case of unemployment, Venus produces better chances to find a suitable position. Health may also benefit from the positive energy of Venus. A pet or domestic animal can be part of the pleasures of life and a source of simple natural enjoyment. The areas represented by the House in Taurus play an important role during this transit.

In House VII

Personal relationships benefit from the positive influence of Venus. It is a period to chose to get married or to engage into an important partnership. The other person involved is also favoured by this transit with pleasant implications for the relationship. Projects involving loved ones seem easier to realise. The areas represented by the House in Taurus play an important role during this transit.

In House VIII

This is a good period to invest in good and beautiful objects or values. Financial transactions are more promising and rewarding. Money is better managed. Opportunities increase gains. Sexuality is enhanced in a creative way. Questions about the mysteries of life motivate the search for the right answers. The areas represented by the House in Taurus play an important role during this transit.

In House IX

Official matters produce positive outcomes. Long-distance travels and contacts with far away places and people are more enjoyable and rewarding. Higher studies are also favoured. Venus makes it easier to obtain better results from less effort. It enhances the philosophical aspect of human relationships. The areas represented by the House in Taurus play an important role during this transit.

In House X (MC)

Venus here increases the potential to succeed thanks to valuable opportunities or to better relations with authority, hierarchy, or clientele. Love can also be a source of motivation to reach a summit benefiting from the positive energy such feeling produces. Creativity favours social or professional success. The areas represented by the House in Taurus play an important role during this transit.

In House XI

This period is likely to be marked by pleasant moments with friends and acquaintances. Social activities are a source of pleasure and satisfaction. Good surprises improve the quality and value of human relationships. Artistic creativity is enhanced and contributes to the pleasure of social interactions. The areas represented by the House in Taurus play an important role during this transit.

In House XII

The past becomes a source of pleasure issued from fond memories of people or places. Venus enhances inspiration and imagination favourable to artists and their creativity. It intensifies the link with the spiritual dimension of life. It is also a period of preparation to the transit of Venus in the Ascendant and its beneficial effect to inner personality and natural talents. The areas represented by the House in Taurus play an important role during this transit.

Lesson 18

MERCURY

Mercury is the closest planet to the Sun. It completes a solar revolution in just under 88 days at an average 58 million kilometres from the Sun. By comparison, the Earth orbit almost three times farther to the Sun at an average 150 million kilometres. In a chart, similar to Venus, Mercury is always close to the position of the Sun. Conjunction are not rare. When Mercury is really close to the Sun (and this rule applies to all other planets) in astrology we say that it is "combust". It means that Mercury's own energy is absorbed by the almighty energy of the Sun. It may therefore be considered less significant. To me, the conjunction has more than one meaning, as explained earlier in this book. The influence of Mercury in a House is interesting to determine the degree of mental energy is put to the service of the areas represented by such House.

However, I have not noticed extraordinary events occurring systematically while Mercury transits a House or when it forms a conjunction with such or such planet or other element in a chart. Perhaps this is because of the proximity with the Sun largely taking over the potential influence of Mercury. Hence, we could consider that Mercury's role is neutral, with some exceptions often due to other transits occurring simultaneously.

Mercury being the ruler of Gemini, perhaps this sign is more sensitive to its influence. It is also the case when Mercury is a dominant planet in a birth chart. In any case, the areas represented by the House where Mercury transits are affected to some degree to be assessed before drawing conclusions on the nature of the transit during the period concerned.

Mercury represents the intellect and the role of the cerebral function in private and social interactions. Communication ability is also shown by the position on Mercury and the aspects with other elements in a chart. Short-distance travel, primary studies, brothers and friends, and common human relations fall under the influence of Mercury. For more information, read my complete astrology course available from Amazon in your country or region[17].

In mythology Mercury is the messenger of the gods. Hence, it represents the link between signs and Houses. We can imagine that Mercury communicates information from one planet to another during its course around the zodiac. A transiting conjunction with transiting Jupiter sextile Venus, when Mercury reaches Venus, it delivers the information that can then be used to derive the benefit of the transiting sextile with Jupiter…

Mercury retrogrades three times during a twelve-month period. While it is in that mode, it is usually not advised to travel, to sign a contract and to get involved in anything that relies exclusively on communication. Moderate but frustrating memory losses are frequent. Mistakes at work, misunderstandings and other setbacks are likely in various types of relationships. The areas represented by the House where Mercury transits may suffer from its retrogradation periods. Keep it in mind in your analysis of the transits of Mercury.

With an average two-week journey through a sign, the messenger of the gods helps understand and communicate or debate about more or less important matters. It may be a propitious moment to make an

---

[17] https://www.amazon.com/s?k=roland+legrand&ref=nb_sb_noss_2

important announcement, to send a letter or email, to make that special phone call, or to catch-up with some friends. Mercury is versatility. It helps us listen, learn, understand, and share thoughts and ideas to connect our neurons with other neurons intelligently.

Next is a series of aphorisms to help you get accustomed to the influence of transiting Mercury.

THE TRANSITS OF MERCURY IN THE HOUSES

In House I (Ascendant)

This period is marked by a stronger need to communicate in a more authentic and spontaneous manner and to express personal thoughts and inner feelings. Mercury enhances the ability to learn and to share acquired knowledge in various ways. The areas represented by the House in Gemini play an important role during this transit.

In House II

Mercury here enhances the necessity to think, to communicate or to reflect about money, revenues, salary, and other daily financial obligations. There may also be more awareness about food and dietary habits and needs. The areas represented by the House in Gemini play an important role during this transit.

In House III

When Mercury transits its "natural House of rulership" its influence is greater in accordance with the energy of the sign absorbed by Mercury. It accentuates the cerebral and neuronal functions. It boosts the intellect. It increases the ability to listen and to learn, and the desire to travel. The areas represented by the House in Gemini play an important role during this transit.

In House IV

This period is usually marked by an increase of communication in the home or about family situations, projects, or events. Travels to visit siblings are more likely and more appreciated. Talks about the place of residence are also more intense, while the areas represented by the House in Gemini play, or not, in favour of the conversations.

In House V

Intellectual and communication skills are addressed to loved ones with a more creative approach. There is a stronger desire to express personal feelings. If travelling is considered, it usually is for a holiday rather than for work. Art can be a source of inspiration. The areas represented by the House in Gemini play an important part during this transit.

In House VI
Contact with co-workers is more intense and often more interesting with Mercury in this House. It is a period to chose to speak out, to send resumes to potential employers, to visit the GP for a medical check-up, or to travel for professional reasons. The areas represented by the House in Gemini play an important role during this transit.

In House VII
Communication in a relationship, marriage or other personal or social partnership is enhanced. There is a need to mentally interact and share ideas and thoughts with others rather than keep opinions personal. Discussing a contract is possible. The areas represented by the House in Gemini play a major role during this transit.

In House VIII
Discussions about money or financial issues are accentuated during this period. The interest in the mysteries of life and death enhances the attraction to occult sciences such as astrology. Talks about inheritance, assets, or investments are likely. The areas represented by the House in Gemini play a major role during this transit.

In House IX
Learning, teaching, or travelling are likely to become a strong source of necessary mental work. Legal matters, ethics, philosophy, and morality trigger a greater need to express, communicate and exchange thoughts and ideas passionately. The areas represented by the House in Gemini play an important role during this transit.

In House X (MC)
The intellect and communication skills can be put to good use to improve the connection with authority or hierarchy. This is a period to chose to present an important project or to express personal ideas, thoughts, and personal expectations. The areas represented by the House in Gemini play a major role during this transit.

In House XI
Interactions with friends and acquaintances enhance social life and the need to intellectually share personal thoughts and ideas with a

larger number of people. Travels to visit friends or to reunite with a place or environment are likely. The areas represented by the House in Gemini play an important role during this transit.

In House XII

Travelling in the past would accurately describe the effect of Mercury here. Retrieving lost items, documents, or people may become a source of great motivation. The connection with the spiritual dimension of life is more important and spontaneous. The need for introspection is also greater and may be linked to the areas of life represented by the House in Gemini during this transit.

* * * * * * * * * *

Remember that Mercury also plays a triggering role. When it forms a conjunction with a slower transiting planet, it enhances the potential to mentally interact with it, and produce important repercussions in the areas represented by the House in the sign ruled by that planet. Mercury delivers messages in accordance with its natal influence in the birth chart.

Chapter 19

THE MOON

The Moon circles around the zodiac in twenty-seven days and six hours. During this period, it forms a conjunction with every element around the chart. The Moon, alike Mars, and the other faster planets, has a triggering effect on events that may have nothing to do with its role in the birth chart. You can easily verify the triggering effect of the Moon by doing a search on meteorological disturbances and natural catastrophes. The dates of these important events often coincide with a significant transit of the Moon.

For example, the full Moon of the 28 February 2010 occurred with the Sun exactly conjunct Jupiter in Pisces. That night, a powerful depression created an unusual storm over the Atlantic Ocean near the French west coast. Cyclone **Xynthia** was an exceptionally violent European windstorm which crossed Western Europe between 27 February and 1 March 2010. It reached a minimum pressure of 967 mb (28.6 inHg) on 27 February. See the drawing below to visualise the effect of the Full Moon when it occurs near major elements in a chart.

According to an article published in a scientific review some years ago, the lunar attraction would be such that it creates a bead of around thirty centimetres on the surface of the Earth, as it orbits around it slowly. The author added that the lunar attraction slows down the speed of revolution of the Earth on its axis by about one second every year. It means that in 3,600 years, the days on Earth will then be 3,600 seconds longer: one hour. Although humans may still consider twenty-four hours to one day, each hour will last two minutes and thirty seconds more that today's hour… The author continued by explaining that sometime in a very distant future, the Moon will be on a stationary orbit around the Earth and only visible from one area of our planet.

Xynthia Cyclone

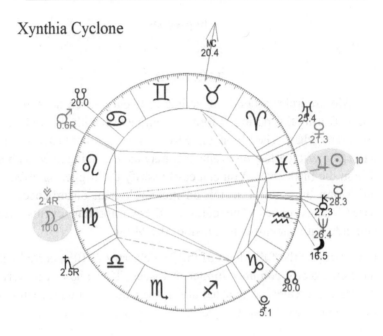

28/02/2010 16:39

There will be no more Full Moons or New Moons as we know them today. Each event will last a much longer time because it will be determined by the orbit of the Earth around the Sun rather than by the orbit of the Moon around the Earth. There will be one Full Moon and one New Moon per year...

In the chart of the Xynthia Cyclone event, note the cluster in Pisces opposed to the Moon and Vesta in Virgo. Vesta: harmony, the Moon: water, Virgo: earth.

Across the chart, the cluster in Pisces shows an enormous mass of water amplified by the almighty energy of Jupiter. Venus and Uranus represent the unexpected force of the storm with its dramatic consequences on human lives who suffered tremendous sentimental and material upheavals.

As another example of the force of attraction and triggering effect of the Moon, see the chart of the of 26 December 2004, when the **2004** Indian Ocean earthquake and **tsunami** (also known as the Boxing Day **Tsunami** and, by the scientific community, the Sumatra–Andaman earthquake) occurred at 07:58:53 in local time (UTC+7) with an epicentre off the west coast of northern Sumatra, Indonesia. 227,898 people lost their lives, not mentioning the immense material destruction. It was another Full Moon day, proving once more, the extremely strong influence of our natural satellite.

Tsunami

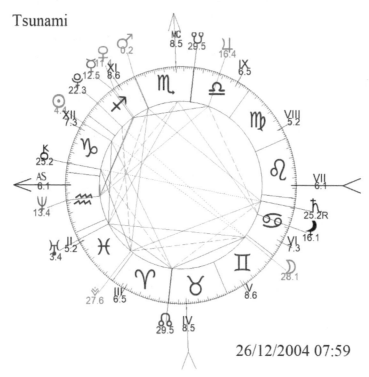

26/12/2004 07:59

The transits of the Moon in Houses have a strong influence when other transiting planets are involved, especially by a conjunction or an opposition. These are kinds of New-Moon and Full-Moon effects.

The Moon produces emotional surges that can interfere with or improve the potential to deal with various events and situations in the areas represented by the Houses concerned during a transit, in relation with the areas represented by the House in Cancer.

The transits of the Moon are likely to have a more remarkable influence in Cancer, in House IV, in the House and sign where it is positioned in the birth chart. The transit through the solar sign is also more significant. Each time it conjunct the position of the Sun in a birth chart, it creates the effect of an eclipse that lay enhance or lower vital energy depending on other simultaneous transits affecting the position of the Sun. For a few hours to a full day, the Moon disturbs physiologically and psychologically, and may open the door to serious disruption if other slower transits confirm such prognosis.

In February 2012, Neptune began a fourteen-year journey in Pisces, its sign of rulership. Every month or so, the Moon passes by the position of Neptune enhancing its natural energy for a few hours before and after the transiting conjunction. Intuition and inspiration may greatly benefit from the combined energies of Neptune and the Moon. However, they can also increase confusion, uncertainty, and emotional disorder with physiological and psychological effects. Neptune intervenes on the hormonal function that the transit of the Moon is likely to disturb or intensify.

The transits of the Moon in the Houses play a role that needs to be observed and controlled to avoid problems or take advantage of opportunities. The psychological effect of the Moon can become a source of emotional outbursts with a variety of consequences. Memorable errors or fits of sheer genius are often triggered by the Moon when it enhances the influence of other transiting aspects around the chart.

Depending on the "size" of a House, the transit of the Moon can last from one to five days. It takes approximately two hours to progress by 1° around the zodiac? and 2.5 days to transit one full sign. These short transits have a more remarkable effect when they join with other transits in the same sign and House.

Determining the exact moment of entry of the Moon in a House depends entirely on the time of birth. The transits of the Moon are often used to verify and/or rectify the time of birth which is rarely precisely quoted. However, as soon as the Moon enters a sign, it starts to influence the House positioned at the beginning or at the end of that sign. It may be more accurate to base the reading on that moment, and then to confirm the influence when the Moon enters the House. The date and time of entry in a sign is found in the ephemerides (or ephemeris) book. Here is an example.

L	1	14:43	♒
Me	3	18:10	♓
D	7	23:43	♉
Me	10	3:01	♊
V	12	8:15	♋
D	14	16:27	♌
Me	17	3:37	♍
V	19	16:15	♎
L	22	3:56	♏
Me	24	12:49	♐
V	26	18:32	♑
D	28	21:53	♒

On the left the days and times of entry of the Moon in each sign of the zodiac for June 1953. Whether a House begins at 2° or 28° in Cancer, for example, the Moon has an effect on the areas represented from Friday 12 June at 8:15 AM GMT (UT) until Sunday 14 June at 16:27 GMT when it starts to transit in Leo.

Because it remains in the preceding House until it reached the cusp of the House in Cancer, the reading must consider all areas concerned by both Houses.

Remember: The Moon acts as a trigger of events produced by slower transits.

Example:

Jupiter transiting the cusp of House II indicated a period of financial evolution in relation with the areas represented by the House in Sagittarius. When the Moon forms a transiting conjunction with Jupiter on the cusp of House II, the moment is propitious to benefit from an opportunity or to request a rise at work. However, it is important to take note of other transits occurring simultaneously.

Contradicting influences from Saturn, for example, would temper the positive influence of Jupiter. That is why I often repeat that a transit rarely acts alone.

As explained earlier in the example about Jupiter, the Moon acts as a trigger or detonator of the latent energy of the giant planet which produces chain reactions leading to more or less important events in the areas represented by the Houses concerned.

Keep in mind that the Moon increases the sensibility to the areas represented by the House transited. It progresses by about 1° around the zodiac in two hours. Its influence on the cusp of a House is active for half a day or so. If the time of birth is correct, the period can be reduced to a couple of hours or less, making this event interesting to take advantage of the conjunction to make an important decision or to take advantage of some opportunities.

We are usually more vulnerable to cosmic emissions when the Moon transits the solar sign, especially when it forms a conjunction with the Sun. Because of its proximity to the Earth and its obvious influence on our planet, many events naturally occur while the Moon is in the vicinity of sensitive areas or elements in a chart. The fact that such events repeat regularly once a month or so since birth creates a habit and resistance to their effects. However, they increase in strength when the transit of the Moon combines with that of another planet or element in the chart. That is another evidence that a transit, if not never, rarely acts alone. Lastly, New Moons and Full Moons seem to have a greater effect than other phases of our natural satellite.

Next is a list of short aphorisms about the possible effect of the Moon in each one of the twelve Houses.

THE TRANSITS OF THE MOON IN THE HOUSES

In House I (Ascendant)

During this short period, the emotional nature of the inner self is more apparent. It may be source of confusion as well as inspiration. Lack of objectivity is however likely to produce uncomfortable situations. Personal feelings motivate sudden mood changes and physiological discomfort. The areas represented by the House in Cancer play an important role while this transit lasts.

In House II

This period is likely to be marked by confusion in finances due to forgetfulness or to and excess of emotional reaction. Compulsive buying, for example, is possible. There is a need to take care of dietary habits to avoid digestive discomfort. However, the Moon can also enhance business flair and culinary inspiration. Areas linked to the House in Cancer play an important role during this transit.

In House III

During this short period, the intellect is likely to be confused by emotions and other sentiments that may distort the ability to think and communicate rationally. It is necessary to increase awareness while driving to avoid incidents due to a tendency to daydreaming or thought wandering. The areas represented by the House in Cancer play an important role while this transit lasts.

In House IV

Family affairs and homelife take a more emotional trend when the Moon transits its "natural House of rulership". It intensifies the need to relate to siblings in a more spontaneous and sensible manner. There is a stronger desire to satisfy siblings that may impair the necessary objectivity to avoid disappointment. The areas represented by the House in Cancer play an important role during this transit.

In House V

This transit increases creativity and the incidence of emotions on the expression of personal feelings with loved ones. The Moon may become a source of inspiration favourable to artists. It is also a period to choose to conceive a child, to get engaged, or to benefit from an unexpected strike of luck. The areas represented by the House in Cancer are linked to the general tendency of this period.

In House VI
Emotions and professional responsibilities do not cohabit easily. Uncertainty at work increases the risk of errors that may be due to health condition. Daily routine is also affected by a tendency to react more sentimentally than rationally. Domestic animals can become a source of emotional excitement or confusion. The areas represented by the House in Caner contribute to the tendency of this period.

In House VII
Emotional outbursts are likely to improve or disturb personal relationships depending on the ability to channel the energy of the Moon to increase creativity and understanding of the other person's needs and expectations. However, moodiness or sulkiness may become a source of occasional disruption. The areas represented by the House in Cancer play an important role during this transit.

In House VIII
Emotional interferences are likely to become a source of misunderstandings about finances. It is not advised to engage in expensive or risky transactions. Sexuality is either enhanced or tempered depending on other elements of the chart and other transits occurring simultaneously. The areas represented by the House in Cancer play an important role during this transit.

In House IX
Official matters, travelling, teaching, studying, or philosophizing is likely to be a source of emotional outbursts due to a tendency to feel more vulnerable due to increased sensibility. Intuition may however enhance the ability to derive greater benefit from unexpected opportunities. The areas represented by the House in Cancer may play an important role during this transit.

In House X (MC)

Personal objectives or ambitions become a source of emotional outbursts issued from a loss or an excess of self-confidence. Personal feelings produce unexpected mood changes that affect peacefulness while enhancing ingenuity to deal with complex and troublesome situations more efficiently. The areas represented by the House in Cancer play an important role during this transit.

In House XI

Enhanced emotional ties with the social environment, both human and geographical are likely. Friends may become a source of elation due to a predisposition to relate to others with accrued sensitivity. Dependence on their approbation, however, may lead to unexpected disappointments or mawkish reactions. The areas represented by the House in Cancer play a significant role during this transit.

In House XII

The past is likely to become a source of emotional excitement and uncertainty. A tendency to feel more vulnerable and to lose self-confidence or self-esteem may lead to various mood changes and inner confusion. Health issues become more apparent and troubling. An effort is necessary to remain rational and peaceful. The areas represented by the House in Cancer play a role during this transit.

Lesson 20

THE SUN

The Sun is the most import element of all. Without it, the solar system as we know it would not exist. We all depend primarily on the energy of the Sun, on its magnetic field, and on its heat. All the celestial bodies in the solar system depend on the Sun to be where they are and what they are. Mercury, Venus, Mars, the Moon, and the other planets feed on solar energy. They absorb it and send it back into space. The Earth intercepts a large part of it with variable impacts on what happens to all sentient beings, plants, and to the weather and other natural manifestations of the Earth reacting to the almighty attraction of the Sun combined to that of the other planets.

The transits of the Sun tend to give life to the elements they come in contact with once a year. The Sun, like the Moon never retrogrades. Therefore, their transits only occur once, contrary to the other planets with up to three times the same aspect during periods of retrogradation.

The transits of the Sun in harmony or discordance with its own position in the chart are quite easy to determine. They occur at exactly the same periods each year. Harmonious transits are a source of natural vital benefit with ramifications in various areas of life. The discordant ones produce disturbances that may be counterbalanced by other transits taking place simultaneously or by your own free-will. They intervene in the areas represented by the House in Leo (ruled by the Sun) and the Houses where the transits occur.

During a transit of the Sun, the other elements in a chart are magnified and intensified by the energy of our central star. **The conjunction is the most influential of all transiting aspects.** It virtually revives the meaning of the planet concerned to give it more energy and intensity. The Sun is light; therefore, its transits allow a more accurate vision of what needs to be done to derive greater benefit from the potential represented by the planet or element affected during the transiting aspect.

14° le 5/12/2016

This person died on 5 December 2016. The Sun in Sagittarius had just begun its yearly transit in House IV, forming on opposition with its original position in Gemini, and with Mercury, Saturn, and Uranus also in Gemini. It formed a square aspect with the Ascendant in Virgo and an inconjunct with Vesta.

This transit of the Sun had a more intense influence than the preceding years because the subject was battling against an advanced form of cancer for a number of months. Since birth, the Sun had transited 73 times in Sagittarius. Each time, it probably dug deeper into the physical resources of this person. On that day, of course, other transits collaborated with the disturbing influence of the Sun.

The transits of the Sun have to be taken into consideration. Astrologers concentrate on slow planets and their long-lasting influences that are a backdrop before which faster transits act like passing comedians in a stage-play.

To forecast a transit of the Sun is easy to do once you remember where each planet, House and other elements are positioned around your birth chart. If the Moon is in Taurus, you know that the affects it during the Taurus period, approximately between 20 April and 20 May. During this period, and more so when the Sun forms a transiting conjunction with the natal position of the Moon, what it represents in the chart is likely to be revived and enhanced. Knowing this fact in advance allows to prepare for the event, either to benefit more from its positive energy or to protect from possible disturbance.

Furthermore, month after month, each House around the chart is energised by the Sun. A stronger effect is likely when the Sun forms a transiting conjunction with the cusp of a House. The influence perdures until the Sun reaches the cusp of the following House, but it lessens when it leaves the sign where the House begins.

The Sun progresses by just under 1° in one day. If a House is 45° wide, the transit lasts 45 days. The transits of the Sun are therefore easy to pinpoint and watch just by looking at a birth chart. It is even easier for those astrologers using the *Equal-House* system of domification, giving each House the same width as the zodiac signs: 30°. I use the Placidus system which considers the size of a House according to the latitude of birth.

The exact time of birth being rarely known, the cusps of the Houses are not 100% sure. That is why it is safer to remain approximative when dating the influence of the Sun or other planet in transiting conjunction with a House cusp.

Here is a list of aphorisms describing the potential influence of the transits of the Sun in the twelve Houses. During these transits, a link is made between the House concerned and the zodiac sign of birth where the Sun comes from. The areas represented by the House in Leo must also be taken into consideration to enrich the analysis of the solar transits.

THE TRANSITS OF THE SUN IN THE HOUSES

House I (Ascendant)

This transit enhances the need to more authentic self-expression. The Sun increases the part of ego to the behaviour in accordance with the zodiac sign of birth. It boosts the natural energy and brightens up the "image de marque" with an effectiveness that depends on other transits and natal configurations involving the cusp of the Ascendant. The areas represented by the House in Leo play an important role.

House II

During this period, money and food seem to be prevailing subjects. Freewill is likely to have a strong influence on the evolution of finances and material life. Light may be shed on the subject of dietetics. However, the Sun can also increase natural attraction to food with no discrimination for what is good or bad for health. The areas represented by the House in Leo play an influential role.

House III

The energy of the Sun is likely to increase the need and potential to communicate. It has a strong influence on the "grey matter" and the intellect. It also enhances the interest in reading, writing, or travelling. Relationships with siblings are also boosted. The ego may however become a source of relationship disturbance. The areas represented by the House in Leo play a key role during this transit.

House IV

Family life, home affairs, or the place of residence become more important and more motivating subjects. There is a need to be more active in both human and geographical environments. The energy and characteristics of the Sun sign of birth intervene more intensely through a stronger expression of the ego. The areas represented by the House in Leo play a major role during this transit.

House V

Creativity is enhanced in various ways. There is a stronger need to express personal feelings. Romanticism favours the evolution of personal relationships. The better side of life seems more accessible.

Holidays, games, and other distractions are a source of positive motivation. Providential events are also likely. The areas represented by the House in Leo play an important role during this transit.

House VI

Work and health are more important during this period. Motivation in stronger and useful to deal with professional missions, duties, and issues. An enhanced sense of responsibility produces better results, but it can also increase tension and anxiety detrimental to wellbeing and physiological balance. The areas represented by the House in Leo play an important role during this transit.

House VII

The ability to collaborate with others or to be more active in personal relationships is stronger. Getting involved in a private, social, or professional partnership is not impossible. However, a tendency to excessive involvement may be detrimental to personal needs due to the opposition to the Ascendant. The areas represented by the House in Leo play an important role during this transit.

House VIII

The Sun produces an accrued attraction to morbid subjects or to the mysteries of life and death. It also increases the ability to invest financially or morally in some important project. Sexual needs are stronger. Rigorous control of strong desires is crucial to avoid bad moral outcomes or financial losses. The areas represented by the House in Leo play an important role during this transit.

House IX

The energy of the Sun enhances the potential to study, to travel, to deal with official or legal matters, and to share personal thoughts, ideas, or concepts with others. Greater interest in foreign countries and cultures is likely. The philosophical approach to life's events is more spontaneously positive and outgoing. The areas represented by the House in Leo play an important role during this transit.

House X (MC)

Evolution of the social or professional status in some way is not unlikely. The Sun at the top of the chart gives personal ambitions greater potential and stronger motivation. However, important projects can be detrimental to family life (opposition with House IV). Meeting in the middle is a must to succeed both ways. The areas represented by the House in Leo play a major role during this transit.

House XI

Social life is boosted by the energy of the Sun. More importance is given to both human and geographical environments. Interaction with friends and acquaintances is intensified. There is a stronger need to help or to be useful to others. Important meetings or encounters can lead to a major partnership or contract. The areas represented by the House in Leo play a major role during this transit.

House XII

The past is somehow highlighted and can become a source of helpful motivation to understand and overcome old issues or obstacles. There is a need to prepare for some important situation or personal project that may take place when the Sun transits the Ascendant. Remaining rational is necessary to avoid Psychosomatic disorders. The areas linked to the House in Leo play a role during this transit.

Lesson 21

THE LUNAR NODES AND LILITH

The Lunar Nodes are determined by the crossing points of the orbit of the Earth around the Sun (ecliptic) with the orbit of the Moon around the Earth. They are known as the South and North Nodes or the Head and Tail of the Dragon. There are other names such as "Rahu" (North Node) and "Ketu" (South Node) for example, and many more, I am sure, from one country's culture to another.

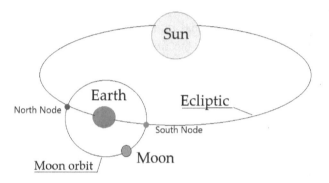

The ephemerides (ephemeris) give their "true" and "mean" daily positions. The true Lunar Nodes move back and forth from retrogradation to direct motion. The mean Lunar Nodes retrograde constantly. They turn around the zodiac clockwise.

I use the mean Lunar Nodes natal positions in karmic readings of birth charts. I also find them useful to complement a forecast based on the analysis of the transits. They are interesting to analyse in Solar Return chart readings as well.

The mean Lunar Nodes take eighteen years to complete one revolution around the zodiac. The event corresponds to a change of cycle, a change of situation or a change of needs and purpose in life.

The South Lunar Node represents what we need to detach ourselves from, while the North Lunar Node is linked to the direction that we should be taking to free ourselves from the tendency to reproduce the same mistakes over and over again.

The transits of the Lunar Nodes act in a very different manner than any other planet or element around the chart. That is because they are always transit together in exact opposition to one-another.

While the North Node shows the way to evolution and success, the South Node increases the need to remain the same. This paradoxical situation underlines our natural tendency to revere and to dread change. The transits in the Houses can last many months to more than a year. These long periods are marked by an urge to progress toward some important goal in the areas represented by the House concerned. As you know, the first six Houses are directly opposed to the six others. House I is opposed to House VII, House II to House VIII, House III to House IX, House IV to House X, House V to House XI, and House VI to House XII.

Opposite Houses complement one another.

House I (Ascendant) is the "I am" House, while House VII (Descendant) is the "we are" House. House II is the "I have" House, while House VIII is the "we have" House. And so on. Opposite Houses depend on one-another to operate properly. House III represents our intellect, while House IX represents what, why, and how we use it for. The paradox is that no mater our IQ, it is useless if we do not put it to good use through studies and social interaction.

The Lunar Nodes highlight the values of opposite Houses and show us how we can take advantage of our potentials in the areas they represent. However, because we cannot have it both ways, we have to choose. The best choice to make is linked to the North Node, and what we need to accept and let go is shown by the South Node.

To make it easier for you to analyse the transits of the Lunar Nodes in the Houses, see the list of aphorisms in the following pages. They are just a glimpse of what can be derived from their combined influences as they circle clockwise around the zodiac.

THE TRANSITS OF THE LUNAR NODES IN THE HOUSES

North Node in House I, South Node in House VII
During this period, the objective is to reinforce personal needs and potential in relation with the inner-self and the inner-truth and detach from the influence of important relationships. Emancipation is in the air. Moving forward implies to let go of slowing factors and concentrate on the goals to reach.

North Node in House II, South Node in House VIII
During this period, the challenge is to reach specific goals in matters ranging from professional or personal revenues, to improving dietary habits and personal approach to material life. Reimbursing loans and other important steps seem necessary and even essential to free from the burden of debts and their negative repercussions.

North Node in House III, South Node in House IX
Why make it complicated when you can make it simple? This is the leitmotiv of this period during which basic intelligence prevails on culture and complex knowledge. Short-distance journeys are more rewarding than far-away travels. Being direct and spontaneous liberates from the burdens of social opinions, rules, and prejudices.

North Node in House IV, South Node in House X (MC)
"Family first" is the motor of this period during which the place of residence, close relationships, and siblings are a source of positive motivation. Social or professional responsibilities need to be clearly assessed and addressed to lighten the burden of personal ambitions with their detrimental influence on the humbler pleasures of life.

North Node in House V, South Node in House VI
"Love is in the air" is likely to be the main source of inspiration and motivation. Creativity promotes intimate satisfaction that needs no approbation nor recognition from anyone out there. Letting go of social prejudices that lock into artificial needs and behaviour allows more freedom from friendship and more independence to live privately what does not require to be shared with others.

North Node in House VI, South Node in House XII

Essential tasks need more attention and care. Work and health are likely to become prevailing values and strong sources of positive motivation. The past may play a retaining or restricting role of which it is essential to let go to avoid getting locked into preconceived ideas and opinions that have no valuable role to play in the future.

North Node in House VII, South Node in House I (Ascendant)

Turning to others for comfort or reassurance is likely to become essential during this period. Rather than remain locked into a supposedly authentic self-centred behaviour, collaborating is a stronger source of motivation and success. Personal opinions are valuable when they can be shared in private or social relationships.

North Node in House VIII, South Node in House II

Rather than solely depend on personal finances that can be limiting and frustrating, collaboration with others is likely to produce better results. Real-estate and other forms of investments are a source of motivation to go forward and upward on the ladder of material wealth. Inheritance is another possible means of enrichment.

North Node in House IX, South Node in House III

Why stay at home or within close surroundings when the world in open to the astute traveller who enjoys discovering new countries and cultures? Learning is the key to make the best use of personal intellectual capacities. Broadening the mind through studies and communication with strangers are sources of pleasure and success.

North Node in House X (MC), South Node in House IV

The need to reach important goals is strong and intensely motivating. Family situations or the place of residence need to be clearly assessed and addressed to free from their restrictive incidence on personal potentials and aspirations. Accepting to fly away from the apparent safety of the nest may be the most effective decision.

North Node in House XI, South Node in House V

Social life, friends and acquaintances contribute to make life more effervescent and interesting. What personal feelings have to give enhances collective realisations. Rather than keep sentiments private and isolated, sharing them with others enriches natural talents and strengthens the link between love and friendship.

North Node in House XII, South Node in House VI

The spiritual dimension of life is a vast invisible area where the soul finds refuge and seeks answers to key existential questions. There is an enhanced need for transcendental freedom and moral elevation that depend solely on the ability to let go of unnecessary duties and obsolete responsibilities. Health is a major factor of realisation.

Use these aphorisms carefully. They are meant as a rough guide. Do not take them for granted. Houses represent multiple areas of life. Use you own common sense to analyse the transits of the Lunar Nodes. Remember that they have a karmic meaning. As such, knowing that no two persons have exactly similar karmas, there cannot be two exactly similar reactions to the influences of the transiting Lunar Nodes.

Lesson 22

LILITH

Lilith is the name given to a area around the Earth called "second focus of the ellipse". The Moon's orbit around the Earth is not a circle, it is an ellipse. The farthest position from the Earth is called the "apogee" (see drawing below) and the closest position is called the "perigee". The Earth is said the be the "first focus" of the ellipse. Lilith is the second focus of that same ellipse. It is positioned according to the movement of the Moon which is in line with the "centre of the ellipse". The same distance from the centre of the ellipse and the Earth is used the opposite way to determine the position of Lilith, also called "Black Moon".

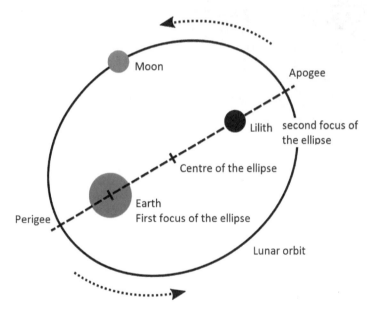

In mythology, Lilith has a bad reputation... Here is a short description taken from Wikipedia...[18]

---

[18] https://en.wikipedia.org/wiki/Lilith

Lilith is a demonic figure. She is first mentioned in biblical Hebrew in Isaiah 34:14, and later in Late Antiquity in Mandaean Gnosticism mythology and Jewish mythology sources from 500 AD onwards. Lilith appears in historiolas (incantations incorporating a short mythic story) in various concepts and localities that give partial descriptions of her.

She is mentioned in the Babylonian Talmud, in the Book of Adam and Eve as Adam's first wife, and in the Zohar Leviticus as "a hot fiery female who first cohabitated with man".

Lilith perhaps originated from an earlier class of female demons in the ancient Mesopotamian religion, found in the cuneiform texts of Sumer, Assyria, and Babylonia.

Lilith continues to serve as a source material in modern Western culture, literature, occultism, fantasy, and horror.

In astrology, Lilith has just as bad a reputation as in mythology. Because there are three possible positions determined by different calculations based on the principle described earlier, Lilith is a question mark. The possible positions are called: true, mean, and rectified. I use the mean position, but you are free to use whichever seems more suitable to you.

Note: there is an asteroid called Lilith in the asteroid belt between Mars and Jupiter. It has nothing to do with the "Dark Moon", the Lilith we are discussing in this chapter.

Lilith represents our dark zones, what we hide, perhaps what we are ashamed of. It has to do with libido and sexuality. It also represents our need to discover and understand the truth about ourselves through hardship and physical or psychological suffering. Its position in a birth chart reveals how and in area of life this problematic energy reigns. Its transits around in the Houses transfer the troubling influence in the areas represented by the House concerned in relation with the areas represented by the natal House position of Lilith. For example, natal Lilith in House IV transiting in House VIII, drags what it represents in House IV into House VIII.

Lilith takes almost nine years to circle of the zodiac. It spends about nine months in every sign. Its transits in the Houses can last more or less than nine months, depending on the "size" of the House. If you work with the equal-house system, this rule does not apply. Lilith remains nine months in every House and in every sign.

Lilith transiting through a House is likely to produce confusion, uncertainty, and perhaps fear of the unknown, or irrational fear in the areas represented by the House concerned. It is there to show what needs to be done to shed light on the dark zones, and to unveil the truth about some of the areas represented by that House. It has a troubling incidence because nothing is clear about Lilith. It also indicates hidden danger motivating adverse reactions that may create paranoid tendencies.

However, to me, Lilith is not that bad… Our hidden potentials, talents, and qualities can emerge during a transit in a House. It enhances our natural ability to search, to dig deep, and to bring to light what has been ignored or somehow dreaded. There is a karmic tinge to the influence of Lilith. What attracts us is not always what we should be attracted to. Understanding that is a great asset when it comes to dealing with our flaws. Only the searcher is likely to find or discover. Lilith drags us to the depth of our inner selves, where the greatest treasures lie unseen. From there, it belongs to us to bring such riches up to brighten up our lives.

Next is a list of aphorisms about the transits of Lilith in each House. Use them to understand that darkness is light, and light is darkness…

THE TRANSITS OF LILITH IN THE HOUSES

House I (Ascendant)
During this transit, an in-depth questioning of the Self is likely to produce a degree of inner confusion and doubt. Sexuality may be a source of attraction to unsafe behaviour with regrettable results. Fear and apprehension of the unknown produces a tendency to withdraw for protection or reassurance which often becomes a source of ambiguity and discomfort in private relationships.

House II
The material side of life is marked by doubts and fear of the unknown. Lilith can affect eating habits and alter their benefit. It can suggest poisoning or intolerance to certain foods. Interaction between money and sex is increased. A tendency to consider money as a negative destructive medium is often observed. The notions of life and death are more present and a source of moral discomfort.

House III
The intellect is more intensely influenced by the mysteries of life and the darker side of earthly existence. Sex may also affect the quality and depth of thoughts and cogitations. However, fear of the dark and of the unknown is a source of interest and attraction. The desire to unveil the truth leads to troubling discoveries about the Self. Accepting flaws and moral weaknesses helps overcoming them.

House IV
Family discomfort or suffering is likely to produce a tendency to darken the existential landscape. Doubt and fears increase the impact of difficult events and situations. They impair the quality of life withing the home and place of residence. They question the true value of belonging and heredity. Dislikes range from family customs to the country's status, meteorology, or geographical situation.

House V
Lilith here produces a tendency to mistake lust for love and to behave with great impetuosity that is likely to have regretful or disappointing consequences. Affectivity is impaired by a deeper attraction to the darker side of life and its troubling effect on the ability to enjoy good times. The expression of personal feelings is influenced by irrational fears and unmentionable motivations.

House VI

Work and health are a source of doubt, suppressed dislike, and disillusion. Fearing the worse increases uncertainty about the future with a negative influence on the quality of daily life. There is a need to investigate deeper into the true motivation behind professional choices and social status. Illnesses are more likely to be the physical expression of psychological or emotional disturbance.

House VII

Lilith here tends to increase physical attraction in marriage and other private personal relationships. It may also create uncomfortable situations outside of marriage such as adultery, although this is often more of a secret sexual fantasy than an eventual reality. Doubt about the other person generates inner anxiety and questioning. It enhances the need to discover together with the fear of what is to be found.

House VIII

If Lilith had a House of rulership, it would be this one where it makes sexual desires stronger than in any other. It produces a need to transcend physical attraction and sexual interaction. It also increases the interest for the mysteries of life and death. It creates a renewed fascination for the darker side of human mentality and behaviour. Finances may become a source of worry and doubt.

House IX

During this transit, dealing with the official side of life, the administration, politics, or the law, is a source of discomfort and worry. Adverse circumstances may be responsible for the emergence of hidden or unforeseen flaws with their troubling consequences. The mysteries of life and death become a philosophical topic that increases inner uncertainty about moral or ethical responsibilities.

House X (MC)

During this transit, uncertainty and doubt reach the highest point, indicating a period of self-questioning about the moral value of social or professional success. There is a stronger need to understand why and how life leads us to always want more. It may create a tendency to deny personal talents and potentials. It also makes it more difficult or awkward to deal with authority and hierarchy.

House XI

This transit announces a period of underlying ambiguity in the social sphere. Friendship tends to be mixed with more intimate feelings motivated by sexual desire and physical attraction. Uncertainty stems from a need to question the ethical value of human relationships and interactions. The geographical environment also contributes to inner doubt and underlying dissatisfaction.

House XII

During this period, Lilith produces an awkward attraction to past events that may have a morbid connotation. Sexuality may be affected by a tendency to seek secret or more intimate impulses. The connection with the spiritual dimension of life is a source of inner questions without answers. The feeling of being in a no-man's land is perceived as a required struggle to reach the hidden truth.

Do not take these aphorisms for granted! They are only meant to give a "feel" of what Lilith may produce when it transits through a House. There are more to them than what is written in six lines of text. Lilith drags us to the bottom, to the darker area of our soul to awake our most ambiguous qualities. There is nothing else to be ashamed of than what you decide is unfair, unethical, or immoral. We all have libido and primitive impulses and needs. Accepting that is like accepting the reptilian part of our brains, the part that developed first, hundreds of thousands of years ago, when only this portion was necessary to ensure our survival…

Epilogue

SYNTHESISING

Forecasting is the art of understanding the combined influences of most of the planets transiting around a birth chart and affecting the same area of life. Blending is a real challenge.

First, always consider a planet in transit from its basic symbolism. The Sun represents the masculine principle, the ego. The Moon represents the feminine principle and emotions. Mercure represents the intellectual principle and communication. Venus represents the love principle and luck. Mars represents the combative principle and action. Vesta represents the harmony principle and balance. Jupiter represents the evolution principle and opportunities. Saturn represents the restricting principle and concrete results. Chiron represents the analysing principle and health. Uranus represents the transformation principle and drastic change. Neptune represents the dream principle and intuition. Pluto represents the regeneration principle, death, and rebirth.

Then, you need to consider the sign and the House where the transit occurs and analyse its potential influence from these two additional points of view.

Next, you have to synthesise the accumulated data from one transiting planet with one more and another until you are satisfied that all relevant elements have been taken into account. You will most certainly notice that some transiting aspects are contradicting.

For example, you may find Jupiter forming a transiting trine with the Ascendant and a square with the Mid-Heaven. And there can be more than two transiting aspects produced by the same planet.

There can also be a transiting trine from Jupiter and a transiting square from Saturn. The best way to determine which of the two aspects prevails it to check the strength of the two planets in the birth chart. Jupiter in Sagittarius is stronger than Saturn in this sign. But Saturn is stronger than Jupiter in Capricorn.

Work out the dominant planet using the planetary chain technique presented in my book: "Astrology for a better life" available from Amazon or from your local bookstore. The dominant planet always produces significant transiting reactions.

The number of transiting aspects from the same planet can be overwhelming. The example chart below shows just how complicated it can be to forecast anything tangible from a single transit…

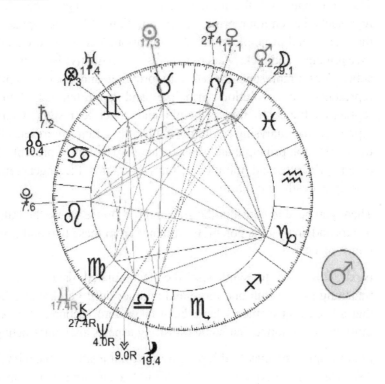

Around this chart, Mars transits in Capricorn. See how many aspects it forms with the natal positions of various planets and other elements. Analyse the influence of this transit may prove quite challenging…

I chose to draw a "Houseless chart" to make it simpler for you to see the number of aspects. However, it is essential to take note of a transit in a House because it allows to locate the influence rather than just explain what it may do. In fact, understanding the meaning of a transit in a House is sufficient to deliver a good description of its impact in the areas represented.

The gathered data open windows after windows on the future, without loosing sight of the past. The past? Yes, because the past is represented by the birth chart around which the transits describe a potential future…

Simultaneously consider a transiting planet from its basic principle and from its sign and House rulership point of view. Jupiter is the expansion and evolution principle, and it also represents the areas of life linked to the House in Sagittarius.

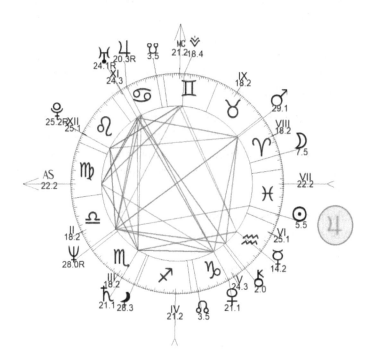

Around this chart, Jupiter transits the position of the Sun in House VI announcing a period of professional evolution. Jupiter being the ruler of Sagittarius, it also rules House IV in this sign. To be more relevant, the forecast must include the notion of evolution together with what family and place of residence can contribute to the expected success derived from the powerful influence of Jupiter.

When a cluster is formed by slow planets transiting in a sign, its global influence can overpower all other transits during the same period. An example is the triple conjunction between Jupiter, Saturn, and Pluto in Capricorn. The event was so rare that it had to announce a historical year. That was 2020… In a video recorded in July 2019 and posted on my YouTube channel, I explained how this conjunction alone was to produce such exceptional reactions. The slow planets have a deeper effect. The slowest is Pluto, transiting in Capricorn between 2008 and 2024. It was first met by Saturn when it entered in its own sign, Capricorn, in December 2018. Jupiter came last and produced the magnifying effect on the other two. Pluto is death, Saturn is restraints and Jupiter is legal regulations… At least this is one way of looking at this great conjunction. The last time it occurred in Capricorn was in 4,574 BC…

Note that the slow transits affect the life of the Earth itself. It produces all sorts of reactions. Meteorological, seismic, volcanic manifestations are provoked by the slower transits when they are met by faster ones and their triggering effect explained in previous chapters.

Analysing the possible consequences of slow transits is interesting in world astrology. The faster planets are more relevant in individual charts. They are useful to prevent disturbances from discordant aspects and to benefit from harmonious ones.

REMINDER

Fast transits trigger events caused by much slower transits.

After a conjunction between a transiting planet and the cusp of a House, a conjunction is possible with a natal element positioned in that House. You must simultaneously consider *the areas represented by the House concerned, the House represented by the transiting planet, and the House represented by the natal planet in the House transited.*

You will need to analyse numerous charts before you can understand how transits work to deliver a comprehensive and useful forecast. At first, be satisfied by simple reading. The more complicated you are, the more mistakes you are likely to make. Forecasting is an art. As such, it requires hours of daily practice. Once you master the instrument, you can improvise and easily navigate on the sea of information contained in an astrological chart.

Astrology is life's weather forecast.

When you analyse the possible influences of the transits to realise a forecast, described them as you would when talking about weather changes. Do not give your reading a definite meaning, something that would be determining and unavoidable. Instead, put free-will first. Encourage and give hope.

From you point of view, explain what the best choice of action or behaviour would be to take advantage of a dissonant transit rather than be a resigned victim of it.

Tell what you would do if you had to deal with a similar transit around your own chart. Implicate yourself to give more credit to your prognosis.

Let the person know that what you describe may not exactly reflect the actual events. There is always another way to look at what is happening. It is a question of point of view. Often, changing our point of view changes the overall meaning and consequence of an event. Put forward the fact that whatever happens is necessary to progress on the spiritual ladder. This present life is the result of our previous existence. It is also preparing us for our next incarnation...

I hope this book will help you progress in the art of forecasting with astrology. It reflects only a fragment of what could be taught about transits. Astrology is constantly progressing. Humility is a requested quality to ensure a sensible approach and a better connection with the elements in perpetual movement around a chart. A know-it-all attitude would certainly result in many errors to the detriment of both the customer and the astrologer. Astrology requires total devotion and an open-mind to grasp its essence and transcend it to the highest level of competence.

Far from being recognised as public utility, astrology is present from the lowest to the highest levels of society. To admit the influence of the Moon is the first step to recognise the possible incidence of the other celestial bodies in the solar system. No form of life as we know it would be possible if the Earth was not exactly where it is around the Sun. The seasons are intrinsically linked to the course of the Earth around the Sun and its fluctuating effulgence. The Earth's climate and the climate of our life are conjointly derived from the organisation or the celestial bodies in the solar system. The unstable balance thus produced is a concrete reflexion of what happens on Earth, for the planet itself and form its occupants, weather changes, seismic and volcanic activity, and other earthly manifestations.

Thank you for your interest in my work.

Roland Legrand - April 2021

Table of contents

Made in United States
Troutdale, OR
09/28/2024

23208298R00156